How Do We Spend Our Time?

How Do We Spend Our Time?

Evidence from the American Time Use Survey

Jean Kimmel
Editor

2008

W.E. Upjohn Institute for Employment Research
Kalamazoo, Michigan

Library of Congress Cataloging-in-Publication Data

How do we spend our time? : evidence from the American time use survey /
Jean Kimmel, editor.
　　p. cm.
　　Includes bibliographical references and index.
　　ISBN-13: 978-0-88099-337-1 (pbk. : alk. paper)
　　ISBN-10: 0-88099-337-5 (pbk. : alk. paper)
　　ISBN-13: 978-0-88099-338-8 (hardcover : alk. paper)
　　ISBN-10: 0-88099-338-3 (hardcover : alk. paper)
　　1. Time management—United States. I. Kimmel, Jean.
　　HD69.T54H665 2008
　　650.1'10973—dc22

2008024108

*Book
$19.00*

The facts presented in this study and the observations and viewpoints expressed are
the sole responsibility of the authors. They do not necessarily represent positions of
the W.E. Upjohn Institute for Employment Research.

Cover design by Alcorn Publication Design.
Index prepared by Diane Worden.
Printed in the United States of America.
Printed on recycled paper.

FSC
Recycled
Supporting responsible
use of forest resources

Cert no. SW-COC-002283
www.fsc.org
© 1996 Forest Stewardship Council

Contents

Acknowledgments

I want to thank the authors for their commitment to this project, and Margaret Coughlin of the Department of Economics here at Western Michigan University for her able handling of the logistics related to the authors' visits to campus. Additionally, I want to acknowledge my remarkable children, David and Lizzie, for their constant reminders of the value of time, particularly the time we spend together.

Introduction

Jean Kimmel
Western Michigan University

Economics is about scarcity of resources and the choices people make in light of that scarcity. Perhaps the most obviously limited resource is time. There are only 24 hours in a day, 7 days a week, regardless of an individual's wealth or power or country of residence. Thus, each of us confronts the necessary choice of how to spend our time.

Economists have long been interested in the analysis of time use decision making. Studies of this nature have been limited until recently by a lack of quality time use data. In 2003, after years of study and preparation, the U.S. Bureau of Labor Statistics initiated the annual American Time Use Survey (ATUS). Each year, a randomly selected subsample of the outgoing rotation group of the Current Population Survey (CPS) will be asked to participate in the ATUS.[1] A randomly selected individual aged 15 or older will complete a 24-hour time diary. In this single-day diary, one adult per selected household describes his or her activities in 15-minute intervals. Reported activities are categorized by an activity lexicon that contains 406 distinct activities. Also provided are data on where the activity took place and with whom. The 2003 ATUS survey sample was the largest, with approximately 40,500 households surveyed. In the following years, the ATUS sample was reduced to approximately 26,000 for cost reasons. In each year of the ATUS, there are an even number of weekdays and weekend days sampled (ATUS User's Guide 2007).

In addition to the detailed time use survey, the ATUS data are supplemented with much of the data available in the CPS. Additionally, researchers have the capability to match ATUS individuals to the full CPS survey data to facilitate the examination of a broad array of time use behaviors across a variety of demographic categories. Although the first ATUS data did not become available to the broader research community until midyear 2005, countless papers have been written to date

1

using the data to analyze everything from time spent with children, education investments, computer use, and shopping.

There is some concern about response rates for the ATUS, as the rates have fallen since the onset of the survey. The ATUS response rate was 57.8 percent in 2003, 57.3 percent in 2004, 56.6 percent in 2005, and 55.1 percent in 2006. However, the concern is more acute for activities that might be correlated with the probability of survey response. For example, Abraham, Helms and Presser (2007) have shown that individuals who volunteer are substantially more likely to respond to the ATUS survey request, thus studies of volunteerism using the ATUS may not produce reliable findings.

Chapter 1, titled "The Time of Our Lives," is written by Professor Daniel S. Hamermesh of the University of Texas at Austin. In this book opener, Hamermesh provides a broad overview of how economists talk about time and how economic analyses of time use can contribute to our understanding of human behavior. Hamermesh begins by aggregating the 406 separate time activities that can be reported on the ATUS into four composite activities: paid work, unpaid work, leisure, and tertiary activities (i.e., necessary activities such as sleep). He notes that comparing across gender in the United States, men and women perform approximately the same amount of total work; that is, the combination of paid and unpaid work. Additionally, while women perform more shopping and caregiving than men, men's time devoted to these traditionally female activities has grown in recent years. Finally, he shows that workers in the United States devote more time to paid work than do workers in other developed countries.

Hamermesh then moves on to examine a variety of topics that can be studied with time survey data. First, he addresses the question of sleep to see if time spent sleeping is related to economic factors such as the individual's hourly wage rate. He finds that, indeed, individuals with higher market wages, other things equal, are likely to devote less time to sleep than those with lower market wages. Then he looks at the timing of work; in particular, the timing of work across the day and the week and across one's life cycle. He shows that workers in the United States perform more paid work on the weekends than do their European counterparts. Additionally, he examines the dramatic change in time allocation observed for individuals at the point of retirement and discusses whether our society might resolve some of its projected future skilled labor shortage by facilitating a transition from full-time to part-time professional work, rather than the current necessity of complete labor force withdrawal. He explains that if fixed costs of work could be alleviated, workers at retirement age might be more likely to transition more gradually to an out of the workforce status, thereby enhancing their own happiness as well as lessening labor shortages.

Continuing on the theme of the timing of work, Hamermesh examines the work timing of spouses to determine if there is any link between leisure synchronicity and income. He finds that higher-income workers are better able to achieve this synchronicity. Hamermesh concludes his chapter with a discussion of the time crunch; that is, which workers are most likely to report not having enough time and why. He explains that it is not possible to outsource much of home production, thus the rich are not able to "buy themselves" out of much of these responsibilities. In other words, it is difficult to substitute goods for time, thus we would expect higher paid individuals to report the greatest time stress. He finds that this appears to be the case, thus the complaints about time are comparable to complaints about having too much money! He concludes this discussion with speculation about why women are more likely to complain about time than men. He suggests that the greater time discontent on the part of women may be due to the fact that they move across a larger number of activities on a single day, and these transitions are costly.

Hamermesh concludes his chapter with a call to arms, so to speak, for economists. While he asserts that "the creation of the ATUS as a continuing survey is the single most important data initiative in the labor area to occur in the 40 years" since he completed his doctoral degree, to exploit this unique opportunity will require that we "think like economists rather than to mimic sociologists."

Time has value. Time removed from one activity to engage in another represents a loss of value of some sort in the original activity. Never has this fundamental point been more clear than with the transference of maternal time from time in the home to time in the paid workforce. As mothers increased their time commitments to the paid workforce throughout the past century, they necessarily withdrew time from unpaid commitments, including housekeeping and caregiving.

The national and even international import of this transference may not seem immediately obvious, but one must look only at the import placed on the measurement of national economic activity to realize that as a once freely provided activity becomes a market purchased good (e.g., purchased housekeepers and babysitters), there are substantial implications for the measurement of economic activity.

Nancy Folbre and Jayoung Yoon, both of the Department of Economics at the University of Massachusetts at Amherst, address this important but complex topic in their chapter titled "The Value of Unpaid Child Care in the United States in 2003." As the authors explain, interest on the part of economists in the value of caregiving extends beyond even concern about measurement of economic activity. Indeed, the care and nurturing of children is the first component in the creation of productive adults. Thus, caregiving is interesting for its human capital investment component because in a sense, children are public goods.

Folbre and Yoon explore two of the difficulties inherent in measuring the value of caregiving: measuring the time involved and assigning a dollar value to this time. Any parent who has been unable to run an errand because he/she is responsible for a sleeping child knows that time devoted to caregiving involves much more than the time one spends in direct interaction. Thus, caregiving is more of a responsibility than an activity. That said, perhaps the best way to capture the full spectrum of caregiving is a time use survey. Using the American Time Use Survey, the authors define a caregiving continuum using increasingly broad measurements for the time devoted to children. These various measures are possible because the ATUS includes information on the respondent's activities as well as information concerning who is present at the time of the activity. Additionally, the ATUS permits caregiving to be reported as a secondary activity. Using these data, the authors construct three categories within the caregiving continuum: direct care (in which the mother is involved directly with her children), indirect care (which includes housework and household management on the behalf of children), and supervisory care (which includes the "nonactive" but responsible minutes of caregiving).

For each of these types of caregiving, the authors assign a monetary value to the time involved based on the replacement cost approach.[2] In other words, the authors assign the dollar value that would have to be paid for someone other than the mother to perform the tasks with or for her children. Along this vein, the most expensive type of care is developmental care; for example, the time a mother would spend reading to her child. The least expensive type of care is simply being responsible for a child who may or may not even be in the same room as the care provider.

Folbre and Yoon conclude that for married women with children under the age of 12, caregiving exceeds the value of their average market earnings. Additionally, the money that parents spend purchasing goods and services for their children is valued less than the time parents devote to their children. As they explain, there are policy implications of the recognition of the substantial value of parental time inputs in their children. Specifically, when time inputs are incorporated, the value of public contributions to child rearing (e.g., tax deductions for children) represent only approximately 4–9 percent of the average cost of raising a child, rather than the 10–25 percent estimated public contribution if time costs are ignored.

As was stated previously, time has value. However, when economists measure economic well-being and produce estimates of inequality, typically time is not considered. Cathleen D. Zick and W. Keith Bryant, of the University of Utah and Cornell University, respectively, focus on the value of out of market time devoted to household activities in their chapter titled "Does Housework Continue to Narrow the Income Gap? The Impact of American Housework on Economic Inequality Over Time." Using the ATUS, they measure unpaid time devoted to household production and compare the current value of this time (relative to total current household income) to previous measures to determine the relative contribution of unpaid time to the total valuation of economic well-being. In order to assess the role that housework has played in economic well-being over time, the authors must explore the changing nature of housework and the role played by the changing sociodemographics over the course of the past 25 years. They describe five inter-related phenomena: 1) the changing nature of women's connection to the paid workforce and their rising educational levels, 2) the increase in the percentage of households headed by a single mother, 3) the changing racial mix in our population, 4) fertility decline, and 5) the increase in the average age of our population. With this discussion of the flux in sociodemographics, they explain the changing distribution of measurable household income. Overall, household income has become much more unequal over the course of the past quarter century.

Once they present and explain the changing distribution of household income, they present estimates of the value of unpaid household production time. They use ATUS data from 2003 along with time use data from the year 1975. They include a broad listing of household activities, incorporating all activities that could be outsourced — that is, all activities that could be performed by a third-party provider. Also, like Folbre and Yoon, Zick and Bryant use a replacement cost approach to derive dollar measurements of the value of unpaid household production in 1975 and 2003. They find that the dollar value of unpaid household work rose dramatically over this period, but increased much more for those with higher household incomes relative to those with lower household incomes. As a consequence, they conclude that overall economic inequality rose from 1975 to 2003 because of an increase in income inequality and due to a worsening in the distribution of the value of unpaid housework. The ability of the value of housework to reduce household inequality has fallen over time.

Zick and Bryant go beyond this conclusion of worsening inequality to determine the role played by changing sociodemographics in this changing distribution in the value of unpaid housework. To do this, they contrast the observed change in income and unpaid housework distribution to what might have been observed had there been no change in the underlying sociodemographic construct of the population. They find that these demographic changes have ameliorated the shift in overall economic inequality. But, despite these sociodemographic changes, they find that three factors have contributed to the increase in overall economic inequality: labor market shifts, technological change in household production, and education-related changes in preferences and opportunity costs.

Jennifer Ward-Batts of Wayne State University extends the discussion of the economic value of household production in her study of retirement titled "Household Production, Consumption, and Retirement." She explains that many studies have documented a decline in consumption among the retired population but that no satisfactory explanation has been offered. She provides one explanation: that the decline in consumption is balanced by a corresponding increase in nonmarket production, thus equalizing the overall value of consumables. Ward-Batts focuses on individuals at pre-retirement age (ages 55–61) and compares their time-use patterns to those who are past retirement age (ages 65–71). She compares time use both descriptively and using regression analyses to control various factors that might affect time choices. Ward-Batts finds some evidence that household production time increases after retirement, more so in total minutes for women than men but more as a percentage of preretirement household production time for men. She concludes that her findings are consistent with the notion that retirees substitute home-produced goods for market-purchased goods.

Moving beyond the issues surrounding the value of out-of-market time, Jay Stewart of the Bureau of Labor Statistics studies the ways that males use their time when they are not employed. As he notes in his chapter, "The Time Use of Nonworking Men," the labor force participation of prime-age males has declined over the past quarter century, but little is known about how these nonworking males are spending their time and how they are supporting themselves. He notes that nonworking males are very likely to have sources of unearned income, with those reporting nonwork due to sickness or disability most likely to report these sources of unearned income. Overall, he finds little variation in sources of income across different groups of nonworking men, concluding that differences in time use are likely to be driven more by preferences than by a relatively greater need for household-produced goods that might exist were income more variable across individuals. Stewart focuses on five broad categories of time use: work-related activities, unpaid household work, leisure, personal care, and other activities. He compares time use for workers versus nonworkers across these five broad categories. He notes that nonworkers spend about an hour more in household production, 90 minutes more in personal care, and four more hours a day in leisure than full-time workers. Much of this increased out-of-market time is devoted to sleep and watching television. Stewart shows that nonworkers do not seem to be replacing market work with nonmarket work because the majority of the time freed up by not engaging in market work is spent in leisure activities.

Stewart constructs an index to measure how dissimilar the time uses are for different types of individuals. Using this dissimilarity index, he shows that retired individuals' time use is quite similar to the time use of individuals with disabilities. Additionally, he shows that full- and part-time workers use time very differently, but that when workers' time use on days they do not engage in paid work is examined, their time use is quite similar to that of nonworkers. Finally, he provides a nice presentation of the differences in time use of nonworkers according to the reasons they report for not working. His chapter concludes with an appendix that contains a fully developed theoretical model to explain what labor economic theory has to say about the differences to expect in time use for workers versus nonworkers.

This volume concludes with the chapter by Anne Polivka of the Bureau of Labor Statistics titled "Day, Evening, and Night Workers: A Comparison of What They Do in Their Nonwork Hours and with Whom They Interact." As the title suggests, Polivka examines the very important issue of work timing across the 24-hour day and how the timing of work impacts our ability to interact with family and friends. Polivka explains that workers are categorized as nonday workers if they worked more than half of their paid work hours outside the day time period 8 a.m. to 4 p.m. According to this categorization, approximately 20 percent of workers report a nonday work schedule, with slightly more than half working in the evening and most of the remainder working a night shift. She notes that those working nonday shifts tend on average to come from more economically disadvantaged situations than those workers with a standard day schedule.

The focus of Polivka's chapter is whether the timing of work affects individuals' health and welfare, and therefore whether a particular work schedule imposes a cost on those workers. To do this, she stratifies the ATUS activity lexicon somewhat differently than the other authors in this volume. She focuses on five broad areas, stratifying by activities related to health, care of home or family, shopping, leisure time, or activities related to paid work. One important finding relates to sleep: she notes that nonday workers actually sleep more minutes a day than do their day working counterparts. Additionally, she notes that nonday workers do not exercise less. She finds that nonday workers spend more time, on average, in unpaid household production but less time caring for family members. Nonday workers also engage in more leisure time, but the bulk of this leisure time is devoted to television. Furthermore, nonday workers spend less time eating and less casual time with family and friends. Polivka concludes her chapter with the finding that evening workers appear to be paying something of a "cost" for that particular nonday schedule, but that the costs associated with a night schedule are not so clear.

Once completing the six chapters of this volume, I hope the reader will agree that the work presented herein succeeds in meeting Hamermesh's challenge to economists to analyze time use data using the best tools and intuition that economics has to offer. At a minimum, the chapters provide the reader with a better grasp of how we spend our time and how economists can utilize time survey data to glean a better understanding of everyday life.

Notes

1. The outgoing rotation group is that group of sample respondents who have recently completed their eighth and final interview for the CPS.
2. The common alternative to the replacement cost approach is the opportunity cost approach which applies the caregiver's market wage opportunity to all time she devotes to her children.

References

Abraham, Katharine G., Sara Helms, and Stanley Presser. 2007. "The Effects of Survey Nonresponse on Inferences about Volunteer Work in the United States." Unpublished manuscript presented at the IZA Topic Week: Nonmarket Time in Economics, held in Bonn, Germany, May 30–June 2.

American Time Use Survey User's Guide. 2007. "Understanding ATUS 2003 to 2006." U.S. Bureau of Labor Statistics, Washington, DC. http://www.bls.gov/tus/atusersguide.pdf (accessed December 5, 2007).

1

The Time of Our Lives

Daniel S. Hamermesh
University of Texas at Austin

Time is the ultimate scarce resource, yet we do not pay enough attention to its scarcity. This chapter presents information on allocations of this limited resource in the United States and elsewhere. More important, however, I wish to illustrate how economics can provide insights into the role of time in our lives. A recent pair of advertisements for Mont Blanc pens shows Johnny Depp (or Julianne Moore) holding a pen and saying, "Time is precious, use it wisely." That expresses the essence of my argument: Time is scarce, and because economics is to a large extent the study of scarcity, we as economists have something unique to offer to the analysis of how people spend their time.

The empirical motivation for much of the discussion is the American Time Use Survey (ATUS). Using those and other data, I demonstrate that in a variety of ways the United States is really a strange country in terms of time. I show in a variety of contexts how men and women differ in their relation to time. I examine when people do things and how that has changed over time, and I discuss an increasingly important policy issue: the relation among time use, retirement, and skill shortages.

The central idea motivating much of this discussion comes from Becker (1965): Time is scarce, in that we all only have 24 hours a day—whether a rich or poor person, or a rich or poor country. Both a rich person and an average person in a rich country have many more dollars to spend per unit of time than does a poor person in a poor country. Now, time by itself is of no use whatsoever. One may lie on the bed and occasionally just look at the ceiling, doing nothing, but mostly we use the things that we buy in conjunction with the time that we have available. We take a vacation and we spend money on hotels and airfare and touring and so on. We have to choose not just how to spend time but how to combine time and goods together. Given that time and goods are used together, it is clear that for higher-income people and in richer countries, time is relatively more scarce than goods. Time scarcity is not a problem if you have little money to spend with the time you have.

One might argue that although there are only 24 hours in a day, people are living longer and thus have more total time available over their lives. As the second column of Table 1.1 shows, that is correct: Over the past half century, the average American's longevity has risen sufficiently to provide 10 percent more years to him/her. Also, these are healthier years and, as Murphy and Topel (2006) show, the health improvements compound the improvements in well-being. The 10 percent extra years of life pale, however, compared to the increase in real incomes, which have tripled on average over the past half century. We have gotten much richer, yet we have not obtained much more time in which to spend our vastly increased incomes.

The same issue pertains to an individual as his earnings increase and time becomes more valuable over the life cycle. This became very apparent to me when I started doing economics in the mid-1960s. Two years after we got married, my wife and I took a two-week vacation

Table 1.1 Real Income per Capita and Life Expectancy at Birth, United States, 1955–2005

Year	Per-capita disposable income ($, 2000)	Life expectancy at birth (years)
1955	9,280	69.6
1960	9,735	69.7
1965	11,594	70.2
1970	13,563	70.8
1975	15,291	72.6
1980	16,940	73.7
1985	19,476	74.7
1990	21,281	75.4
1995	22,153	75.8
2000	25,472	77.0
2005	27,340	77.8

SOURCE: *Statistical Abstract of the U.S.*, various issues.

camping in Nova Scotia and New Brunswick, Canada. We drove our beat-up car, stayed in campgrounds, and did our own cooking. In 1989, when my wife was practicing law and I was very busy, we took a one-week vacation to France, staying at good hotels, eating at one-star restaurants and, of course, flying across the Atlantic.

HOW WE (AND OTHERS) USE TIME

What people actually do with their time in this country can be seen using the ATUS. Because the basic data are coded into 406 categories, I, like anyone else using them, must decide about appropriate aggregation. I have combined the activities into four particular types. Table 1.2 shows that on a typical day in 2003, men are working for pay for about 313 minutes and women are working for pay for 201 minutes. The next category, household production, consists of things like shopping, cooking, cleaning, washing the dishes, and child care, i.e., all the things that you might pay somebody to do for you. You could have a cook, a shopper, a cleaner, and a babysitter. We call these activities home work, unpaid work, and other things. As the table shows, women are doing much more of these than men, which is no surprise. Tertiary activities are anything that you must do some of—sleep, wash, eat, and others;

Table 1.2 Average Time Allocations, by Category, United States, 2003, All Respondents Ages 20–74 (minutes per representative day)

	Men	Women
Market work	313	201
Household production	163	271
Family care	28	60
Shopping	43	59
All work	476	472
Tertiary time	616	641
Sleep	496	511
Leisure	348	327
Radio/TV	160	134

SOURCE: Burda, Hamermesh, and Weil (2008).

sleep accounts for the bulk of such time. Lastly, leisure includes things that you do not have to do but that you do for fun. There are slight differences by gender, with women spending more time sleeping, washing up, cleaning up, etc., and men spending more time in leisure. Men work more in the market, women work more at home, but the sums of market and home work, and thus the sums of tertiary activities and leisure, are almost identical across genders.

Although the data are not strictly comparable, it is worth examining how time spent in the critical activities, shopping and child care, has changed in the United States by gender. As Table 1.3 shows, and as we already saw for 2003, it is no surprise to find that women are spending more time in these activities than men. The most recent year's data for child care may be problematic, but certainly between the 1960s and 1990s women were spending less and less time taking care of kids. Partly this is because more women are working for pay, but also (and related to rising female wage rates and labor force participation) there were fewer kids. The average household was producing 3.5 kids in the 1950s, today that number is down to 2. It is worth noting, however, that men and women are sharing more of the shopping and child care, whether as cause or effect of women's increased labor force participation.

Let us compare the United States to other countries. Burda, Hamermesh, and Weil (2008) make similar calculations to those in Table 1.2 for Germany, Italy, and the Netherlands, which are presented in Table 1.4. The thing to note is that we work more for pay than the average adult in these European countries. I could have included many

Table 1.3 Minutes per Day in Shopping and Child Care, by Gender, All Respondents Ages 19–64, 1965–2003

	1965	1975	1985	1992–94	2003
			Shopping		
Men	36	44	46	36	40
Women	61	64	57	56	59
			Child care		
Men	14	13	14	8	12[a]
Women	54	37	27	20	32[a]

[a]Probably defined more broadly than in earlier surveys.
SOURCE: Harvey (2006).

Table 1.4 Average Time Allocations (minutes), Women and Men, All Respondents Ages 20–74, Germany, Italy, and the Netherlands

	Germany 2001–02		Italy 2002–03		The Netherlands 2000	
	Female	Male	Female	Male	Female	Male
Market work	133	263	133	290	124	254
Household production	312	174	347	115	268	145
Family care	42	18	39	19	51	17
Shopping	66	49	53	33	53	36
All work	445	437	480	405	392	399
Tertiary time	675	654	593	595	659	634
Sleep	509	499	499	497	524	504
Leisure	320	349	367	440	389	407
Radio/TV	100	135	89	114	99	119

SOURCE: Burda, Hamermesh, and Weil (2008).

other European countries—even Japan—and we would still find that the average person does not work as much in the market as the average American does. Since these calculations fail to account for vacation time, and since our vacations are shorter than those in other economies (Altonji and Oldham 2003), they understate the excess of paid work here compared to other rich countries.

Comparing across gender in Tables 1.2 and 1.4, consider the total of unpaid work in the household and work for pay. In the three Anglo-Saxon countries, total work time is almost identical by gender—the differences are 2 percent or less. Only in the Mediterranean country do we find the popular expectation—that women do more work in total than men (and implicitly have less free time)—to be true (even though the fertility rate in Italy is among the lowest in Europe). Whether this equality is a general phenomenon and what causes it are things that I am now actively engaged in studying.

INCENTIVES FOR COMBINING TIME AND GOODS

The relationship between goods inputs and time inputs into an activity is unclear. Averaging across all activities, there can be no relationship, as each person spends the same total amount of time—24 hours—on the activities he or she engages in. So the answer depends on whether, relative to the average activity, goods and time are more or less readily substitutable in the particular activity in question. If they are not, we will observe a positive relationship between goods purchased and time spent. Figure 1.1 examines this issue for food spending and time inputs into food (shopping, cooking, eating, and cleaning up). The

Figure 1.1 Relation between the Natural Logarithm of Annual Food Expenditure and Time Spent Shopping for and Preparing Food, Eating and Cleaning Up, U.S. 2003–2004 (horizontal axis is minutes per day, vertical axis is $ per year)

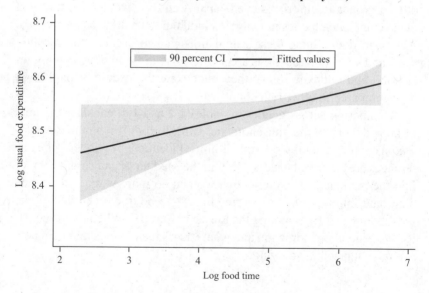

NOTE: 90% CI is the 90% confidence interval around the predicted values of the logarithms of food spending at the logarithms of time spent on eating, food preparation, clean-up, etc.
SOURCE: Hamermesh (2007).

data are for ATUS respondents in 2003 and 2004 matched to the Food Security Supplements in the December 2002 and 2003 Current Population Surveys (CPS). The figure shows that households that spend more on food also devote more time to all the aspects of eating. (This holds even if we adjust for family composition.) This suggests that it is fairly difficult to substitute goods for time in the particular activity of eating.

As Tables 1.2 and 1.4 show, by far the biggest single activity in which people engage is sleep. Is sleep an economic activity—does it respond to economic incentives—or is it purely biologically determined? Taking earlier research (Biddle and Hamermesh 1990), one can use results from the 1975–1976 Time Use Study to calculate for men and women the *ceteris paribus* effect of higher wages. Dividing human activity into only three categories—sleep, market work, and everything else—the first row of Table 1.5 shows time allocations for men and for women whose time price is half the average for their gender. The middle row shows these at the average wage, and the bottom row presents time allocations for people earning twice the average wage. People with higher wages (or potential earnings) sleep less. I would argue that this occurs because the alternative to sleep—working for pay—is relatively more advantageous for them. Indeed, when the unpublished version of this paper circulated, the *New York Times* ran a story about it with the headline, "Sleep? Why? There's No Money in It" (Passell 1989). People have things other than sleep that they can do with their time, and one of those, market work, becomes more attractive when the returns to it rise.

The effects of higher wage rates on time spent sleeping are not so large for women as for men, suggesting that, perhaps for biological rea-

Table 1.5 Effects of Wages on Time Spent Sleeping and in Other Unpaid Activities, United States, 1975–1976 (minutes per representative day)

	Men			Women		
Wage is:	Sleep	Other nonwork	Work	Sleep	Other nonwork	Work
Half the average	495	595	350	494	710	236
Average	487	605	348	497	698	245
Twice the average	469	628	343	503	672	265

SOURCE: Calculated from Biddle and Hamermesh (1990).

sons, the marginal value of sleep for the average woman exceeds that for the average man. Of course, we find the usual result that women's market work time is more responsive to changing incentives than that of men; but the response is all along margins of household production and leisure, and hardly at all along the margin of sleep time. The main conclusion, however, is that even something which one might believe is not responsive to economic incentives—sleep—reacts just the way that economists might expect.

WHEN WE DO THINGS

A widely held notion is that people are now working around the clock in this country—a 24/7 economy. The virtue of time-diary data, such as those comprising the ATUS, is that one knows exactly what each

Figure 1.2A Timing of Work over the Day, Men, 1973 and 2003

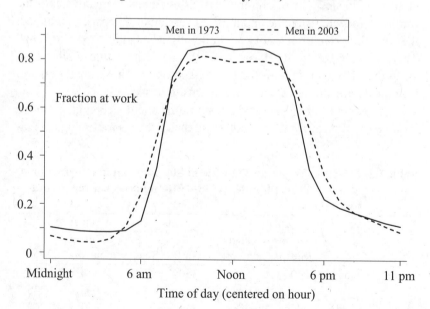

SOURCE: Calculations from Hamermesh (1999) and raw data.

sample respondent is doing at each point in the day. One can, therefore, summarize the fractions of the population engaged in specific activities in each time interval—for our purposes, during each quarter-hour of the day. Included in the calculations here are all those people who work for pay on the diary day, with male and female workers in Figures 1.2A and 1.2B respectively. The data for 1973 are based on the May 1973 CPS Multiple Jobholding Supplement (Hamermesh 1999), which included questions about starting and ending times of market work, while the 2003 data are from the ATUS. In each figure the total amounts of work time have been adjusted to be equal, so that the figures isolate the effect of differences in the distribution of the timing of market work across the day.

Not surprisingly, most of the work for pay is performed in the middle of the day, with very few people working at 3 a.m. The interesting thing to note here is that, from midnight to 6 a.m., the line for 1973 lies above that for 2003 among both men and women. Thirty years ago we

Figure 1.2B Timing of Work over the Day, Women, 1973 and 2003

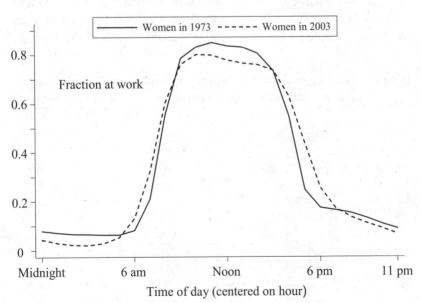

SOURCE: Calculations from Hamermesh (1999) and raw data.

were doing a greater fraction of our work late at night, and similarly for the late evening hours on the right-hand side of the figures. We were also working more during the middle of the day. The big change is not that we are working at night more than before; we are not. Rather, we are performing a much greater fraction of our work at fringe times—early morning, 5–8 a.m., and early evening, 5–7 p.m.

We make decisions about timing over the day, but we also make decisions about timing over the week, the year, and a lifetime. While major chunks of the literature in applied micro- and macroeconomics have dealt with the last of these temporal decisions (essentially looking at life-cycle choices about labor supply), very little has been published on the first of these (but see Hamermesh [1996]). To demonstrate the potential importance of this issue, in Table 1.6 I present information on the hebdomadal distribution of market work by gender in the same four countries for which information was given in Tables 1.2 and 1.4.

What stands out in this table, beyond the fact that I have already demonstrated how much market work Americans do, is how much work we perform on weekends compared to northern Europeans. Indeed, even compared to Italian men we do a greater share of our total market and household work on weekends. Coupled with the fact that Americans have fewer days of vacation than do citizens of the wealthier

Table 1.6 Time Allocations, All Men 20–74, Weekdays and Weekends Separately, Four Countries (minutes per representative day)

Activity	Day	Germany 2001/02	Netherlands 2000	Italy 2002/03	U.S. 2003
		Men			
Market work	Weekdays	340	333	357	392
	Weekends	67	57	124	112
All work	Weekdays	512	471	467	538
	Weekends	245	217	251	318
		Women			
Market work	Weekdays	173	161	165	257
	Weekends	33	33	55	63
All work	Weekdays	503	443	519	522
	Weekends	299	265	383	351

SOURCE: Burda, Hamermesh, and Weil (2008).

European nations, it is clear that we tend to spread our work temporally much more than in other rich economies.

One aspect of life-cycle behavior has been especially heavily studied, namely, retirement/labor-force withdrawal. To me the most interesting aspect of the issue is why people retire—why they go from working full or nearly full time to no market work at all. The incentive effects of Social Security and pension benefits, both labor supply phenomena, have been studied extensively. I want to concentrate instead on incentives resulting from what goes on inside the household—how older people spend time and the effect of working in the market on their allocation of nonmarket time.

As an academic I am very lucky: At any time from my early sixties on I can partly retire—teach half-time or less during the academic year for a set number of years—but retain my job. I could teach full time one semester and have the other eight or more months to do other things, including travel and uninterrupted research. I would receive half my salary and keep my office. There are very few other jobs where a worker can do this. The inability to retire partially in the same job is a problem, because there is an increasing number of highly skilled people who retire fully. At a time when most developed countries are facing or will face increasing skill shortages, partly caused by demography, this loss of older skilled workers seems increasingly serious. Given that older people are healthier at a given age than were earlier older cohorts, policies that inhibit partial retirement or, indeed, that fail to offset incentives for full retirement, implicitly lead to the early destruction of human resources.

To begin, consider how the allocation of time changes over the life cycle. Table 1.7 presents averages by age of time allocations on a typical day for ATUS respondents in 2003 and 2004. Comparing the data for all respondents 55–59 to the same data for all people 65–69, whether they work for pay or not, we see that this decade is where the big drop-off in time spent in market work occurs: A drop from 256 minutes on a typical day down to 87 minutes. Where do these nearly three hours of time go each day? Family care and other household production rise a little bit, maybe 40 minutes a day, and sleeping and eating also rise by around 30 minutes. The big change is in the consumption of leisure, with nearly

Table 1.7 Time Use by Age, United States, 2003–2004 (minutes per representative day)

Activity	<55	55–59	60–64	65–69	70–74	75+
Market work	256	258	178	87	51	14
Other household production	146	187	198	221	225	204
Family care	67	40	49	46	38	32
Tertiary						
Sleep	513	492	505	515	528	543
Personal care	46	50	49	48	46	49
Eating and drinking	68	79	84	88	94	93
Leisure						
TV watching	142	165	189	218	230	250
Other	192	158	175	202	213	236
Other	10	11	13	15	15	19

SOURCE: Donald and Hamermesh (2007).

two-thirds of the time freed up from market work going into leisure—and over half that amount going into additional television viewing.

The question is: Would people possibly enjoy life more, and would society get more out of its highly skilled work force, if people could intersperse leisure and work in a more even pattern over their lives? There is substantial evidence (Gronau and Hamermesh forthcoming; Hamermesh 2005) that temporal variety rises with income at the daily and weekly levels, so why not at the level of the life cycle? One possibility is that there are fixed costs of working just a little bit that cause disruptions to our scheduling of nonwork activities. For example, I need to wear a tie to teach, I need to wash up, I have to socialize with people whom I might not like, my mind is on work even when I am not working that day, etc. Working a little bit disrupts our lives and affects how and when we do our nonwork activities. Does a person who works a little bit behave differently from someone who does not work at all? Does labor force entry affect how people spend time away from work?

I take the 2003 and 2004 ATUS data and estimate how time spent in each of household production, tertiary activities, and leisure is affected by minutes of market work and whether one works, adjusted for a wide variety of demographic characteristics. Using those results, in Table 1.8 I simulate how the typical American adult would spend her time if she did no market work, worked for pay just one minute, did the average amount of work, or worked full time. Of course, the average person, or the full-time worker, spends less time in leisure and less time in household production than nonworkers: There is an adding-up constraint of 1,440 minutes per day. The crucial finding, however, is the difference between the nonworker and someone who works only a little bit for pay. The results show that labor market entry causes one to shift one's nonmarket activities around, consuming less leisure and engaging in more household production. Implicitly the fixed cost of market work induces people to alter their nonmarket behavior.

In the last seven or eight years, people 65 and older have been working just a little bit longer. The reversal of the trend toward reduced labor force participation among older workers is not due to the stock market decline in the early part of this decade (Coile and Levine 2006), nor is it due to increases in the age of eligibility for full Social Security retirement benefits, because that happened more recently. Perhaps it is because people have begun to realize that they need to work more than 40 years to support a retirement that could well last 30 years. Perhaps, however, companies and workers have begun to see the benefits of restructuring work so that older people can enjoy the benefits of variety and their employers can make continued use of their skills.

Table 1.8 **Average Daily Minutes by Paid Work Status, Ages <60, United States, 2003–2004 (minutes per representative day)**

	Market work	Household production	Tertiary activities	Leisure
Nonworker	0	324	675	429
Just one minute of work	1	341	679	407
Average person	263	234	620	313
Full-time worker	343	203	602	280

SOURCE: Calculated from Donald and Hamermesh (2007). Eleven minutes per day could not be classified.

Timing does matter, but how we time our activities is subject to choice, and an interesting question is, What timing is desirable? One aspect of desirability is whose timing is the same as one's own, and the most important person in many people's lives is their spouse. I thus examine who gets to spend time with his or her spouse. This is an economic decision: Although we want to spend time with our spouses (if not, presumably they would not be our spouses for long), spending time with them is costly. It constrains one's flexibility in earning income, so that synchronizing one's schedule with one's spouse's time is costly. Assuming, as seems reasonable, that the fixed costs of scheduling are independent of time prices, and assuming that spousal time is superior, we should find that higher-income couples spend more time together. The spouses take jobs that might not be quite as good as possible in order to spend time together. They still earn a lot more than others, but not as much more as they otherwise would. In other words, one of the extra benefits the rich get out of life is more of the desirable good, time with one's spouse.

Using the CPS May Multiple Jobholding Supplements, I examine for 1973 and 1978 combined, and for 1991 and 1997 combined, the timing of work among couples with two working spouses. In each case I have controlled for the total hours that each works for pay, so that the calculations abstract from differences in the *amount* of labor supplied to the market. If each spouse, for example, works 8 hours per day for pay, it is possible that they could have 16 hours to spend together. Or, however, their schedules could be completely disjointed so that they only have potentially 8 hours to spend together. The calculations are presented in Table 1.9. Going from a couple with each spouse in the tenth percentile of earnings to one with each spouse in the ninetieth percentile shows a small but clear increase in the amount of overlap in their

Table 1.9 Joint Leisure among Full-Time Working Couples, 1970s and 1990s (hours per day)

Hourly wage is:	1970s	1990s
10th Percentile	13.0	12.3
Average	13.2	12.5
90th Percentile	13.4	12.8

SOURCE: Calculated from Hamermesh (2002).

work schedules. Couples in the upper part of the earnings distribution have roughly an extra half hour a day potentially to be together. While this is not a huge amount, it is about 5 percent of the average amount of time not accounted for by market work. This finding suggests that, if we measure well-being based solely on incomes, we understate inequality, since higher-income households have foregone some earnings in order to obtain schedules that allow potentially for more joint leisure.

Couples do schedule themselves very much together; they tend to work in a nonrandom way at the same time and be off at the same time. Hamermesh (1996) shows this to be the case both in the United States and in Germany. Indeed, there is only one demographic group in which the spouses' schedules appear to be completely independent. Not surprisingly, that is couples with young children: If both work for pay, one is likely to be at home taking care of the children while the other is at work. Most couples, however, tend to schedule much of their work time simultaneously, more so than one would expect if this process were random.

HOW WE FEEL ABOUT TIME—AN ECONOMIC APPROACH

Most of us feel that we do not have enough time. Given the limitations discussed in this chapter's introduction, this is not surprising. As economists, we can use the simple insights discussed there to study feelings about being pressed for time and use that study to weigh the importance of such complaints. Time is relatively scarce for higher-income people—partly because their time is more valuable due to market alternatives, partly because they have more income to spend in the same amount of time as the poor, and goods and time are not perfectly substitutable in generating outcomes that increase our happiness. If this is true, we should find the rich complaining more about being rushed for time.

I proposed this idea to a large U.S. foundation whose staff were mostly psychologists and sociologists. The staffers felt that this idea was typical economists' nonsense, responding, "Can't the rich simply have lots of time by paying people to do all the work for them at home that they otherwise would have to do?" In other words, as a wealthier person, I can have somebody clean my house, maintain my garden, install halogen light bulbs, etc., and thus generate lots of time for myself. The answer is a resounding no, because the number of things that I can outsource is really very small. I cannot outsource my sleeping. Nobody can eat for me, attend a symphony for me, or watch the Super Bowl for me. Given this difficulty in substituting goods for time, we should expect more whining about feeling rushed by members of wealthier households.

In each of four countries' large national surveys, respondents were asked how often they feel pressured for time. In Australia, Germany, and the United States, five answers were possible: 1) always, 2) almost always, 3) sometimes, 4) almost never, or 5) never. In Korea only four responses were possible. The distributions of the responses in the four surveys are shown in Table 1.10. Clearly, in each country a large fraction of adults view themselves as rushed much of the time; and very few feel themselves under time pressure only infrequently.

Is the theory of time and goods as joint inputs into utility consistent with what we observe about the impact of income differences on people's feelings about being pressured for time? Consider Figures 1.3A and 1.3B, which present information for men and women, respectively, for the four countries. Each bar presents average household earnings for a particular response to the time-stress question, moving from left to right for each sample from the second most time-stressed group to the least time-stressed group. For comparison purposes earnings are set equal to 100 in each sample for those who say they are always stressed for time—the most time-stressed group—and they are not included in

Table 1.10 Percent Distributions of Time Pressure, Couples—Australia 2001, Germany 2002, United States 2003, and Korea 1999

Under time pressure:	Australia		Germany		United States		Korea	
	Men	Women	Men	Women	Men	Women	Men	Women
Always, almost always	43.4	50.5	34.3	36.4	42.6	54.5	70.7	68.5
Sometimes	41.9	39.3	38.2	41.7	33.5	29.8		
Rarely, almost never, never	14.7	10.2	27.5	21.9	23.9	15.7	29.3	31.5

SOURCE: Hamermesh and Lee (2007).

the graph. Numbers below 100 indicate that a group's earnings are less that of the most time-stressed group.

In most cases, as one moves rightward from the darker bar to the successively lighter bars in Figures 1.3A and 1.3B, average household earnings decrease. Those who express less time stress are those who are earning less. The same result holds when we adjust for how much time people work for pay—the phenomenon arises from differences in time prices, not only from differences in total income. When people complain about how rushed and stressed their life is, they are really complaining that they have lots of money. If they are upset, they could choose to work less and earn less; that they do not choose to work less suggests that, despite the complaints, their utility is higher in the more stressed situation. Indeed, and not surprisingly in light of the theory, those who express more stress for time also are more likely to be satisfied with their income. The poor complain about lack of income, because income is relatively scarce for them, and the rich complain about lack of time, because time is relatively scarce for them. I am more sympathetic to the former set of complaints, but others may have different values.

Table 1.10 also documents a difference in feelings of time pressure by gender: In all countries except Korea, women are significantly more likely to feel that they are rushed for time. (Korea is different from the others because women are much less likely than men to engage in market work, a major source of time pressure.)

Why do women feel more rushed for time? It is not due to the presence of children at home, as the same gender difference exists when one adjusts for the presence of children and even for the time spent in caring for them. One possible explanation is that there are costs of switching among activities—fixed costs of changing what we do—that lead to feelings of being rushed. In six countries, Australia, Germany, Israel, the Netherlands, Sweden, and the United States, Gronau and Hamermesh (forthcoming) examine the number of different activities engaged in on an average day by married men and married women. In each case wives did more different things than their husbands, which could lead to feelings of being rushed. Another possible explanation is that, beyond the additional uses of time in which women engage, they are also managers of the household—they are on call for problems. Yet another, related possibility is that these difficulties combine with fixed costs and rigid scheduling to impose tighter constraints on women's use of time.

Figure 1.3A Household Earnings by Time Stress (earnings = 100 if always stressed)

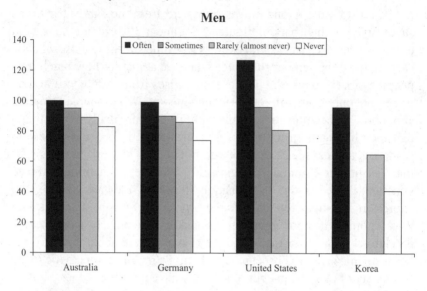

Figure 1.3B Household Earnings by Time Stress (earnings = 100 if always stressed)

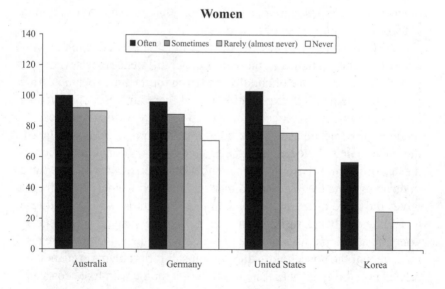

SOURCE: Hamermesh and Lee (2007).

CONCLUSION

The creation of the ATUS as a continuing survey is the single most important data initiative in the labor area to occur in the 40 years since I completed my doctoral degree. Over time it will provide enough information on small demographic groups to allow analyses of the nonmarket behavior of nearly any group in which researchers are interested. It will enable us to chart how time use varies over the life cycle and the business cycle. One caveat is in order, however: Other social scientists are as capable as economists at summarizing allocations of time and making simple comparisons. Our comparative advantage lies in going beyond this to creating interesting theory-based hypotheses that can only be tested with the kind of data on nonmarket time that the ATUS generates. The ATUS should be a boon for economic research, but it also challenges us to think like economists rather than to mimic sociologists.

References

Altonji, Joseph, and Jennifer Oldham. 2003. "Vacation Laws and Annual Work Hours." *Federal Reserve Bank of Chicago Economic Perspectives* 27(3): 19–29.

Becker, Gary. 1965. "A Theory of the Allocation of Time." *Economic Journal* 75(299): 492–517.

Biddle, Jeff, and Daniel Hamermesh. 1990. "Sleep and the Allocation of Time." *Journal of Political Economy* 98(5): 922–943.

Burda, Michael, Daniel Hamermesh, and Philippe Weil. 2008. "The Distribution of Total Work in the EU and US." In *Working Hours and Job Sharing in the EU and USA: Are Europeans Lazy? Or Americans Crazy?* Tito Boeri, Michael Burda, and Francis Kramarz, eds. New York: Oxford University Press, pp. 13–91.

Coile, Courtney, and Philip Levine. 2006. "Bulls, Bears and Retirement Behavior." *Industrial and Labor Relations Review* 59(3): 408–429.

Donald, Stephen, and Daniel Hamermesh. 2007. "The Time and Timing Costs of Market Work, and Their Implications for Retirement." NBER Working Paper No. 13127. Cambridge, MA: National Bureau of Economic Research.

Gronau, Reuben, and Daniel Hamermesh. Forthcoming. "The Demand for

Variety: A Household Production Perspective." *Review of Economics and Statistics* 90(3).

Hamermesh, Daniel. 1996. *Workdays, Workhours, and Work Schedules: Evidence for the United States and Germany.* Kalamazoo, MI: W.E. Upjohn Institute.

———. 1999. "The Timing of Work over Time." *Economic Journal* 109(452): 37–66.

———. 2002. "Timing, Togetherness and Time Windfalls." *Journal of Population Economics* 15(4): 601–623.

———. 2005. "Routine." *European Economic Review* 49(1): 29–53.

———. 2007. "Time to Eat: Household Production under Increasing Income Inequality." *American Journal of Agricultural Economics* 89(4): 852–863.

Hamermesh, Daniel, and Jungmin Lee. 2007. "Stressed Out on Four Continents: Time Crunch or Yuppie Kvetch?" *Review of Economics and Statistics* 89(2): 374–383.

Harvey, Andrew. 2006. *Nonmarket Production and Historical Time-Use Data: Potential and Issues.* Yale Program on Nonmarket Accounts, Yale University, New Haven, CT, May.

Murphy, Kevin M., and Robert Topel. 2006. "The Value of Health and Longevity." *Journal of Political Economy* 114(5): 871–904.

Passell, Peter. 1989. "Economic Watch: Sleep? Why? There's No Money in It." *New York Times*, August 2.

2

The Value of Unpaid Child Care in the United States in 2003

Nancy Folbre
Jayoung Yoon
University of Massachusetts, Amherst

Economists have long recognized that nonmarket work, including time spent raising children, has economic value. Conventional measures of gross domestic product, based only on market transactions, understate the total value of goods and services produced. As women have entered paid employment and reallocated time away from the home to the market, measures of gross domestic product have increased simply as a result of this accounting convention.

The difficulties of measuring and assigning a monetary value to nonmarket work have discouraged efforts to include it within economic accounting frameworks. But many national statistical agencies are now collecting regular time-use diaries from representative samples of their populations. In 2003, the United States became a part of this trend, with completion of the first round of the American Time Use Survey, which will now be administered annually as part of the Current Population Survey. In 2004, the National Academy of Science (NAS) published the report of an expert committee considering methods of valuing nonmarket work (Abraham and Mackie 2004). This report urged economists to develop the tools needed to produce a set of satellite accounts estimating the total value of nonmarket work.

The report raises a number of important conceptual issues, among them the need to move beyond valuation of housework toward a more detailed analysis of care devoted to children as an input into the "human capital" sector of the economy. Valuation of care is more difficult than valuation of housework for two reasons. First, it is more difficult to measure the amount of time devoted to it, which includes supervision and "on-call" time that may not involve direct interaction with a child (Budig and Folbre 2004; Folbre et al. 2005). Second, it is difficult to specify a market substitute or replacement wage rate for work that has strong emotional valence and includes valuable person-specific skills.[1]

In this chapter, we use data from the ATUS to address these two issues. We build upon two recommendations made by the NAS study: that valuation for the purpose of national accounts be based on replacement cost (rather than opportunity cost), and that replacement cost be adjusted, where possible, for the quality of the services required. Because the ATUS is an adult-centric survey, we focus on the development of a measure of adult inputs into children.[2] We draw from a previous paper comparing three distinct measures of child care in the 2003 ATUS for married or cohabiting persons living in a household with a child under the age of 6 but no child over the age of 12 (Folbre and Yoon 2007).

The first section motivates the need to measure time devoted to children. The next section explains why time devoted to children cannot be defined simply as time engaged in primary child care activities. Moving beyond a distinction between primary and secondary child care activities, it makes the case for a "care continuum" that includes both supervisory and housework/management services. Data from the 2003 ATUS demonstrate the relative importance of these different categories of care for the average person age 18 and over. The final section addresses valuation issues and applies different wage rates to the different types of care. Even a conservative lower-bound estimate shows that the average value of time that adult women devoted to child care in 2003 exceeded the value of their average market earnings.

WHY MEASURE TIME DEVOTED TO CHILDREN?

Parents and other family members devote a substantial amount of time and energy to raising the next generation. This work is not primarily motivated by a desire for pecuniary gain, but it has important pecuniary consequences for employers, citizens, and society as a whole. If parents did not raise children, schools would be unable to educate them, and the employers would be deprived of both labor and what has come to be termed "human capital." Governments would be unable to borrow money based on anticipated tax revenues from the next generation.

While parental labor does not come with a price tag attached, its supply seems to be affected by shifts in relative prices. Fertility has declined along with economic development in many parts of the world, and fertility rates well below replacement levels in countries such as Italy, Spain, Japan, and South Korea have raised concerns about adverse macroeconomic consequences.

From a neoclassical perspective, one might argue that parents simply have different preferences than other adults. Some adults choose to spend money and time on children; some adults choose to spend money and time on Golden Retrievers. If children are simply consumption goods, expenditures on them are irrelevant to adult standards of living (Ferreira, Buse, and Chavas 1998). But the standard of living of children themselves is relevant (Bojer and Nelson 1999). Further, children represent public goods, since governments can levy a claim on their future earnings and retirees depend on goods and services produced by the younger working-age generation (Folbre 2008). Even if one accepts the notion that children are merely consumption goods, parents may want to know more about their time costs, and policymakers may wonder what will happen to the supply of children as the cost of raising them goes up.

The time that parents devote to children costs money. Following a recommendation made by Margaret Reid in 1934, most time-use researchers define work as an activity that someone else (a "third party") could be paid to perform. This definition departs from the neoclassical definition of work as an activity that generates no utility apart from the income or services that it may yield. Adults in general and parents in particular often derive considerable satisfaction from child care. Yet they also derive considerable satisfaction from paid work. Time-diary studies that ask respondents to describe their effect and mood indicate that adults, on average, enjoy time with children only slightly more than paid employment. Housework is consistently ranked lower than either (Kahneman et al. 2004).

However work is defined, it seems inconsistent to measure the amount of money that adults spend on children and to ignore the value of the time devoted to them. Money expenditures are consistently monitored. Since 1960, the U.S. Department of Agriculture (USDA) has provided estimates of average expenditures on children from birth through age 17. A recent USDA report estimates that a middle-income, husband-and-wife family with two children spends about $165,630 to raise each child up to age 18 (Lino 2001a). The report itself calls attention to the omission of any estimate of the value of parental time from this calculation.

Foster care reimbursement rates, child support awards of noncustodial parents, and standards of public assistance for poor families are often judged by comparison with estimates of average money expenditures on children (Folbre 2008; Lino 2001b). Both custodial parents and children may be economically penalized as a result. Estimates based on the Child Development Supplement of the Panel Study of Income Dynamics (CDS-PSID), a survey of children ages 12 and under, show that a lower-bound replacement-cost estimate of the value of parental time is higher than the value of cash expenditures (Folbre 2008). That is, direct money expenditures represent less than half of the total cost of raising children.

The United States provides substantial subsidies for parents, easily overlooked because they are embedded in a complex (and ever-changing) tax code. In 2000, the value of tax exemptions and credits was higher, on average, than the Swedish family allowance per child.[3] U.S. subsidies, however, have a far more unequal impact. Unlike the family allowances provided by the social democracies of Northwest Europe— or those provided by the other major English-speaking countries, the United Kingdom, Canada, and Australia, the U.S. tax code provides its greatest benefits to affluent families. Families in the middle of the income distribution receive the lowest level of support (Battle and Mendelson 2001; Folbre 2008).

Unlike most other affluent countries, the United States fails to provide paid parental leaves from work or universal child care. These policies have a direct impact on parental time allocation, making it more difficult for families to balance paid work and family work. Levels of "outsourcing" of child care and shift work are almost certainly higher as a result (Freeman and Schettkat 2005; Presser 1994, 1995). Analysis of the value of parental child care time could have implications for the analysis of such policies.

The valuation of time could also put levels of public support for parenting in a new perspective. Tax subsidies provided in the United States in 2000 amounted to between 10 and 26 percent of the average annual parental expenditures on a child under 18 in a middle-income, two-parent family in that year (Folbre 2008). But once the lower-bound replacement value of parental time is taken into account, the public contribution appears much smaller, amounting to between only 4 and 9 percent of average costs.

HOW SHOULD TIME DEVOTED TO CHILDREN BE DEFINED?

The ATUS provides an opportunity to provide detailed estimates of the time that adults devote to children. But the measurement of child care inputs is more difficult than it may seem initially. Primary child care activities represent only a portion of the temporal burden that children impose. The ATUS asked respondents to record time that children were "in their care," which amounts to a much larger quantity of time than care activities such as feeding, bathing, or talking to children. But how, exactly, should such time be counted? Even the sum total of primary child care activities and "in your care" time omits some important categories of supervisory time and ignores important differences in the intensity and complexity of care needs. Analysis and valuation of child care time should instead focus on a spectrum or continuum of types of care.

Beyond Activities

Most time-use surveys are categorized in terms of activities. But child care is more than a mere activity. It is also a responsibility. As Reid explained in 1934, "Even though she [the household worker] may not be on active duty, evidence of her labor is about her; she is continually on call. Much so-called leisure has a "string attached" (Reid 1934, p. 319). Supervisory responsibilities are the string that constrains both maternal labor force participation and leisure time.

Primary activities are those designated in response to a question such as, "What were you doing during this time period?" The recent Australian and UK surveys designated secondary activities in response to questions such as, "Were you doing anything else at the time?" Extensive analysis of the Australian data reveals the tremendous significance of child care as a secondary activity (Ironmonger 2004). Unfortunately, measures of child care as a secondary activity are highly sensitive to definition and survey design: the ratio of child care as a secondary activity to care as a primary activity is much higher in the 1997 Australian than in the 2001 UK survey (Folbre and Yoon 2007).

The ATUS did not ask respondents to report secondary time use. Rather, the U.S. Bureau of Labor Statistics decided to follow the example of Canada, which had begun administering a time use survey that asked respondents to specify the amount of time they spent "looking after children." The U.S. Bureau of Labor Statistics devoted considerable attention to cognitive studies of the impact of alternative wording and recommended a different phrase, asking respondents to specify the amount of time that children were "in your care" (Schwartz 2001). This question was asked of respondents living in households with children age 12 or under. As might be expected from the broader wording, which reaches beyond the passive or generic care implied by "looking after" to the more diffuse responsibility of "in your care," the ATUS measure yields significantly higher estimates of parental time commitment than the Canadian survey of 2001, even though measures of primary child care activities are quite similar (Folbre and Yoon 2007).

The ATUS "in your care" measure is often referred to as a secondary activity. Indeed, the ATUS itself refers to "secondary care" in its published tables. But this term is misleading, since "in your care" does not designate an activity but rather a responsibility. The term "passive" care is also inappropriate. Many of the most important primary child care activities are in fact rather "passive"—such as watching television with a child or driving a child to school. The ATUS "in your care" measure is best described as a measure of responsibility for children, an indicator of supervisory constraints. Some might view this as a flaw in the ATUS, since it limits comparability with other surveys. But it is also a great strength, because it tells us far more than other surveys about the larger temporal demands that children impose.

The ATUS collected additional detailed information from respondents on who else was present. When the activity was taking place in the home, the question specified, "Who else was present in the same room?" Our analysis of these data clearly demonstrates that adults could and did describe children as "in your care" even when children were not in the same room. Among married or cohabiting adults living in a household with a child under the age of 6 but no child over the age of 12, a child is listed as present for only 68 percent of all "in your care" time (Folbre and Yoon 2007). It is also important to note, however—and probably surprising to most time-use researchers—that children are frequently absent during some primary child care activities. This is especially true of the managerial/logistical activities coded in the ATUS, such as "organizing and planning for household children" (children present only 62 percent of the time) or care-related travel for household child (children present only 74 percent of the time) (Folbre and Yoon 2007).

How Should "In Your Care" Be Counted?

The difference between the amounts of time devoted to activities of child care and time that children were "in your care" looms quite large. Even for those who might be expected to spend large amounts of time in primary child care activities, such as married or cohabiting women without paid employment living in a household with a child under the age of 6, child care activities average only 3.2 hours per day. Time during which a child was "in your care" averages an additional 9.5 hours per day for this group (Folbre and Yoon 2007).[4] In other words, "in your care" time is about three times higher.

The ratio of care activity time to "in your care" time is about the same for the broader category of all women age 18 or older living in a household with a child age 12 or under but no child over that age.[5] Their time in child care activities averages 2.4 hours per day compared to 7 hours per day with children in their care. For men in this category, however, "in your care" time is nearly five times greater. Their care activities average only 0.92 hours per day compared to 4.4 hours with children "in their care."

A significant portion of "in your care" time overlaps with other nonmarket work activities such as cleaning house (women age 18 or older in a household with a child aged 12 or under average about 2.1 hours per day of such overlapped time; for their male counterparts, about 0.5 hours per day). The remainder of "in your care" time overlaps with activities that are not designated as nonmarket work, such as socializing with friends or engaging in leisure. Yet the use of this time is constrained by child care responsibilities. As several studies show, women's leisure is structured differently than men's for precisely this reason (Bittman and Wajcman 2004; Mattingly and Bianchi 2003).

The conceptual dilemma is painful: leaving "in your care" time out seems incorrect, but including it all can lead to double-counting of unpaid work. Furthermore, the intensity of "in your care" is obviously lower than the intensity of direct activities of care.

In a recent estimate of the total value of nonmarket work based on the 2003 ATUS, Frazis and Stewart (2004) offer a reasonable compromise. They tally only the hours of "in your care" time that did not overlap with other nonmarket work activities. Even restricted in this way, "in your care" time is substantial, amounting to about one quarter of all nonmarket work.

We modify and build on this approach in several ways, making use of the information available in the ATUS on the range of different care activities or the presence of other adults or children. We describe "in your care" time as supervisory time (conforming to 1c of the care continuum shown in Table 2.1) only if it did not take place while also performing nonmarket work (as do Frazis and Stewart). However, rather than making a sharp distinction between housework and child care, we argue that some housework represents an indirect form of child care. Children clearly increase the burden of domestic chores and household management tasks. Counting only direct expenditures of time on children would be analogous to counting only parental spending on toys and education, while ignoring the impact of children on rent, utilities, or grocery bills.

Indeed, the ATUS codes seem inconsistent in their effort to measure time spent organizing, planning, and traveling on children's behalf while ignoring time spent cooking or cleaning on children's behalf. This inconsistency could even introduce a class bias, since educated affluent parents are likely to devote more time to such managerial care—and less time to domestic work—than less-educated, low-income parents

Table 2.1 The Child Care Continuum[a]

1. Supervisory Care
1a. Children asleep, adult "on call" but asleep *(not measured in ATUS)*
1b. Children asleep, adult "on call" but awake *(measured in the ATUS only if children are asleep during the day, in which case it is covered by the "in your care" question)*
1c. Children awake, adult "on call" but awake *(measured in the ATUS for children ages 12 and under by the "in your care" question. Also measured by ATUS primary activity code "looking after household children")*

2. Indirect Care
2a. Housework on behalf of children *(not distinguished from other housework in the ATUS)*
2b. Household management on behalf of children *(not distinguished from other logistical and managerial work in the ATUS, although some child-specific categories are included)*

3. Direct Care
3a. Physical care such as feeding, bathing, and dressing *(measured in the ATUS by primary activity codes)*
3b. Developmental/educational care such as talking with, instructing, reading aloud, or playing with child *(measured in the ATUS by primary activity codes)*

[a] Data availability in the ATUS in parentheses; for detailed codes see Appendix 2A.

(Lareau 2003). Even a rough estimate of the proportion of housework and household management attributable to children is preferable to completely ignoring such indirect care.

Most uses of the "in your care" measure exclude time that children are asleep during the night, which represents a substantial portion of supervisory time. Children under the age of 3 spend about half their time asleep; the percentage of time they spend awake increases steadily with age (Folbre et al. 2005). Exclusion of the bulk of sleep time gives the misleading impression that young children require less care than older ones. This is not true, because young children's sleep is often fitful and periodic. They tend to wake at regular intervals and demand brief but highly inconvenient attention.

The teenagers that are omitted from consideration by the "in your care" measure impose rather different demands. They require less direct supervision than children ages 12 or under. Yet precisely because parents spend less time in care activities with teenagers, the amount of time that they are "on call" or "available" may have an important impact on their children's health and education outcomes. Certainly many parents feel constrained by the need to keep an eye on their teenagers.

The Care Continuum

As a first step toward exploiting the full potential of the ATUS, we move beyond the simple dichotomy between child care activities and "in your care" by describing a continuum based on the intensity of effort and potential impact of parental education and skill. This continuum ranges from supervision (which may impinge to varying degrees on adult activities) to housework and household management services to primary care activities.[6] Each of these forms of care can be subdivided in a similar gradation (see Table 2.1). Supervision may take place while both child and adult are asleep, while the child is asleep but the adult is awake, or while both child and adult are awake. Housework involves somewhat routine activities such as food preparation and laundry, while household management services such as negotiation with teachers and doctors can require more effort and skill.

When housework and household management activities on behalf of children are combined with responsibilities for children "in your care," they are more demanding than when children are absent (representing a form of joint production). We do not count time that adults are engaged in housework or household management for themselves in conjunction with children "in their care" as supervisory time, primarily because we want to provide a conservative lower-bound estimate of joint housework/supervision time.

Direct care ranges from physical care (such as feeding or dressing a child) to developmental care with a high level of social interaction (such as talking to, instructing, playing with, or reading aloud). In future efforts we may disaggregate further.

We use ATUS activity codes, information regarding presence of children, and estimates of the housework demands of children to provide an empirical picture of this care continuum. Most, but not all, of the primary activities coded by the ATUS fall into the third category of Table 2.1. Some of these seem out of place to us. For instance, both ATUS activity codes "Looking after Children" and "Caring for Or Helping Children Not Elsewhere Classified" seem designed to capture passive care that is largely supervisory. They consume relatively little time (less than 6 minutes a day, on average, even among married or cohabiting individuals living with a child under 6 but none over 12), but for the sake of consistency, we allocate these codes to category 1c of "supervisory" care along with measures of "in your care."

Another reallocation concerns ATUS primary activity codes "Organization and Planning for Children," "Activities Related to Children's Health," and "Activities Relating to Children's Education," and "Travel." These activities add up to a larger amount of time, almost 20 minutes per day on average. In our view, if children are not present, these should not be considered primary care activities, and we reallocate these segments of time in which no child is present (about 20 percent of the total) to child-related household management.

Estimation of the amount of time devoted to housework and household management on behalf of children is less straightforward. To some extent, these activities provide a household public good. All household residents presumably benefit from vacuuming the living room, cleaning the toilets, or preparing common meals. Other activities, such as doing children's laundry or picking up their toys, are child-specific, but the survey does not record "for whom" the activities were performed. Multivariate analysis can be used to estimate the impact of children on the amount of time devoted to housework (Craig 2005), and we plan to explore this approach at a later date.

However, parents may reallocate their housework and household management time to meet the needs of children rather than adults. Even if they spend the same amount of time as nonparents in these activities, their individual standard of living may suffer as a result. For instance, parents may prepare peanut butter sandwiches instead of adult meals, or they may pick up toys rather than vacuum their own bedrooms.

One simple approach, mimicking the approach the Department of Agriculture takes with money expenditures (Lino 2001a), is to allocate housework and household management time on a per capita basis. The total amount of time devoted to these activities, divided by the number of household members, times the number of children, could be interpreted as the amount of indirect care time devoted to children. Since children represent about half of all household members in households in which adults are living with children, we assign 50 percent of housework and household management activities to children. Our estimates show that about 30 percent of this time is combined with children "in your care," which is tabulated separately because this joint production is more demanding.

Table 2.2 shows amounts of time devoted to different categories in the care continuum for adults (individuals over 18) in three different types of households, those with children under 13 but none older, those that include children ages 13–18, and those with no children. Not sur-

Table 2.2 Average Adult Time Devoted to Children and Paid Employment in the United States in 2003 (hours per day)

	Households with child <13 but none older		Households with child >12		Households with no children	
	Men	Women	Men	Women	Men	Women
Supervisory care (partial measure)[a]	4.0	5.1	0.5	0.8	0.2	0.3
Indirect care	0.6	1.5	0.5	1.3	—	—
Housework (not combined with supervisory care)	0.2	1.1	—	—	—	—
Housework combined with supervisory care	0.1	0.3	—	—	—	—
Household management (not combined with supervisory care)	0.2	0.3	—	—	—	—
Household management combined with supervisory care	0.1	0.1	—	—	—	—
Direct care	0.9	2.3	0.2	0.4	0.0	0.0
Physical care	0.4	1.3	0.1	0.2	0.0	0.0
Developmental care	0.5	1.0	0.1	0.2	0.0	0.1
Average total time devoted to child care	5.5	8.8	1.1	2.5	0.2	0.5

[a] Based on category 1c in Table 2.1.

prisingly, adults living in households with young children devote substantially more time to caregiving than those without. The conventional measure of time devoted to child care activities suggests only a modest time commitment: less than an hour a day for men and about 2.3 hours a day for women. Indirect care time in the form of housework and household management services on behalf of children is slightly smaller for both men and women, at 0.6 and 1.5 hours per day. Supervisory time is much greater in magnitude: small amounts are provided by households with older children because younger children are present; even adults living in households without children provide some supervisory care.

Taking all three large categories of care into account offers a somewhat different picture of the gender division of labor. Men's contributions to household management and supervisory care partially compensate for their relatively small contributions to direct care. In households with young children, women spend about 2.5 times more than men in direct care activities. Inclusion of less intensive forms of care yields a lower ratio of 1.6.

A closer look at variations in the care continuum by other dimensions of household structure (such as marital vs. nonmarital, single vs. two-parent) could yield further insights. We do not disaggregate further because our purpose here primarily is to illustrate this methodological approach and to provide an aggregate picture of the total amount of time devoted to unpaid child care.

ESTIMATING THE MARKET VALUE OF CHILD CARE TIME

The care continuum is well-suited to the application of a range of wages reflecting the replacement cost of different types of care. Supervisory care, often combined with other activities, is less demanding than indirect care, which in turn is less demanding than direct care. However, the choice of specific wage rates to value inputs of care time is, at best, a rather crude exercise, one that can offer only a lower-bound estimate of the value of family time. A number of caveats deserve careful consideration.

Care Provided vs. Care Received

Valuing time devoted to care is not the same as valuing actual inputs of care. Apart from the obvious point that quality of care may differ by individuals and circumstances, differences in the density of care are relevant. An adult who reports spending an hour of time engaged in child care may be the only person in charge of three children, or may be assisted by two other adults in caring for one child. An adult-centric survey that simply tallies hours supplied will show the same result: one hour of care time. However, a child-centric survey will show that three hours of child care are consumed in the first case, but only one in the second case.

Care has many of the features of a household public good. It is not perfectly rivalrous in consumption. In other words, when one adult cares for two children, the care each receives is surely more than half what they would receive if cared for alone. Yet economies of scale, or improvements in efficiency achieved by caring for more than one child at a time, are limited. Care quality is almost certainly diluted as the ratio of children to adults increases. Many time use surveys, including the ATUS and the Child Development Supplement of the Panel Study of Income Dynamics, include questions about who else was present that make it possible to calculate the density of care, or the ratio of adults to children (Folbre et al. 2005). The implications of density, however, are difficult for economists to interpret.[7] Developmental psychologists need to tell us more about the production function for the creation of happy, healthy, productive adults.

Market Substitutes?

The economic logic of the "third-person principle" is easily misapplied. Families are often willing to purchase child care as a substitute for their own time, but only up to a certain point. Developmental psychologists emphasize infants' needs to form attachments with primary caregivers. Some studies of the impact of long hours of institutional care on infants suggest that it can have adverse implications on children's abilities for self-regulation (Brooks-Gunn, Han, and Waldfogel 2002). While these studies are limited by the difficulty of controlling for either the quality of parental or institutional care, most researchers (and surely most parents) would agree that there is a level of institutional care that is "too high." Care is an input not only into the capabilities of a child, but into the quality of an adult's relationship with that child.

The person-specific nature of many care tasks means that no market replacement is a perfect substitute. The hypothetical exercise nonetheless demands consideration of the quality of replacement time. Most estimates of the time cost of parenting—unlike most estimates of the value of housework—rely on opportunity cost—the value of the time that parents reallocate from paid employment in order to care for children, normally proxied by their actual or estimated wage rate (Calhoun and Espenshade 1988; Robinson 1987). Recent estimates focus on the impact of maternal reductions in labor supply not merely on current but on lifetime wages (Budig and England 2001; Joshi 1990; Waldfogel 1997).

Calculation of opportunity cost of time withdrawn from paid employment is an interesting and important exercise, but it is typically used only to capture an estimate of foregone earnings, with no consideration of foregone leisure or household production time diverted from adult consumption. It also provides a better estimate of the value that individual parents place on their own time with children than its social value. In more technical terms, it includes the value of utility a parent derives from a child—a consumers' surplus. National income accounting is based on market prices, not "willingness to pay." (For more discussion of this point, see Abraham and Mackie [2004].)

One way to motivate calculation of the "social" rather than the "individual" value of family care time is to consider the metaphor of a family strike. If parents, grandparents, and other family members decided to withhold their care services from children for one day, what would it cost to provide replacement services of comparable quality?

Comparable Quality

Three factors are particularly relevant to the specification of "comparable quality": density of care, skills of caregivers (partly a function of education and experience), and emotional attachment (partly a function of length and continuity of the care relationship). Comparable density implies care services at approximately the same level of density currently provided. That is, children could not simply be moved into institutional facilities with a low ratio of adults to children. This condition is easily satisfied by calculation of existing inputs of adult care time.

Comparable skills imply that where skill is likely to make a difference to child outcomes, as in the provision of developmental care, the replacement wage should be calibrated to represent services of similar quality. Parental education has a positive and significant impact on outcomes for children (Grossman 2003; Leibowitz 1973). Parental education does not, however, operate in isolation. Comparable attachment implies that wages should be sufficiently high to elicit a long-term commitment with low turnover rates. High turnover rates of employees in paid child care facilities are generally considered an indicator of low quality (Whitebook and Sakai 2003).

Neither of these conditions of comparable skill and comparable attachment is easily satisfied. While it is clear that parental education benefits children, matching the educational level of parent and parent-replacement for a subset of care tasks offers only illusory precision. It is virtually impossible to estimate the wage that would elicit the desirable level of attachment. As a result, we settle for estimates of replacement cost that do not fully meet the comparable quality criterion, simply assigning different values to forms of care that are in different places on the care continuum.

Table 2.3 lists the wage rates that we assign to different types of care, along with a brief description of the rationale behind each wage rate. These are conservative estimates, ranging from a low of $5.15 per hour (the federal minimum wage) for supervisory care to about $25.00 for developmental care. These wage rates are low compared to the average for all paid work in 2003 of $17.41 per hour.

The Value of Child Care Services

We focus on the valuation of time provided by individuals living in households with children 12 or under, since measures for other categories are even more incomplete.

Application of the wage rates in Table 2.3 to the average hourly amounts of different types of care provided by men and women pro-

Table 2.3 Hourly Replacement Wage Rates for Different Categories of Care (matched with similar occupations)

Type of care	Wage rate ($ per hr.)	Similar occupation: avg. wage ($ per hr.)
Supervisory care	5.15	Federal minimum wage
Indirect		
Housework (not combined with supervisory care)	8.00	Maid/janitors: 7.98
Housework combined with supervisory care	12.00	Maid/janitors: 7.98 + 50%
Household management (not combined with supervisory care)	15.00	Mgr. in social and community service: 23.77 – 30%
Household management combined with supervisory care	20.00	Mgr. in social and community service: 23.77
Direct		
Physical care	10.00	Child care worker: 9.00
Developmental care	25.00	Kindergarten teacher: 24.78
Avg. hourly wage across all occupations	17.41	

SOURCE: Pay estimates are from the Bureau of Labor Statistics, 2003.

vided in Table 2.2 are multiplied by 365 to yield annual estimates. The value of the child care time that women in these households provide comes to about $33,000 per year; the value that men provide to about $17,100 per year. Since women in these households tend to perform more intensive forms of child care, the average hourly value of their care services is higher than that of men: $10.27 per hour compared to $8.61.

One way to assess the validity of these estimates is to compare them with the market value of the closest approximation of the entire package of child care services—a nanny. The Bureau of Labor Statistics does not collect information for this occupational category, but a survey conducted by the International Nanny Association (2004–2005) collected 671 responses.[8] Since respondents were largely self-selected, the results were probably biased upward. Nonetheless, it is interesting to note that the average annual pay reported for nannies that did not "live in" and receive part of their pay in the form of rent earned about $30,680 per year. Considering that employers, for the most part, offered Social Security benefits in addition to wages, and that parents continue to spend considerable time with children even with a nanny on the job, this estimate seems reasonably close to the estimate we offer above of the value of women's unpaid child care services.

The range of activities that nannies reported among their "duties and responsibilities" also seems consistent with the range included in estimates here: child care (99 percent); driving (78 percent); organization of children's toys, clothing, and other belongings (77 percent); taking children to play dates (75 percent); laundry (70 percent); and meal preparation (64 percent). The survey also indicates the relevance of a form of supervisory time omitted by the ATUS: 85 percent of surveyed nannies who "lived out" reported that they were paid extra if they were required to stay overnight.

Most women living in households with children ages 12 and younger combine their care work with paid employment but are working for pay on average only 2.7 hours per day (compared to 5.2 hours a day for men). At an average pay of about $15.56 per hour, women earn, on average $15,335 per year. The value of their child care services is more than twice as high. The combined value of their paid work and unpaid care services comes to $48,335. Adding in the value of their non-child-related housework and household management at the same wage rates indicated in Table 2.3 yields an additional value of about $5,402 per year (far less than the value of their child care services). The total average value of work they perform comes to about $53,737 per year. Adding men's average annual earnings of about $43,198 plus $2,519 of non-child-related housework and household management to the value of their child care services yields about $62,817.

Women living in households with children under age 12 are devoting 70 percent of their total work hours to children. Since the replacement value of most of this work is quite low, the overall market value of their total work is low. Inclusion of supervisory care also gives a boost to estimates of the value of men's total work, since they devote about half of their total work hours to this activity. Again, supervisory care makes men look good. This may be a misleading result, since men are probably more likely to report children "in their care" when many other adults are present at the same time. Other studies show that fathers are much less likely than mothers to spend time alone with children (Folbre et al. 2005).

DIRECTIONS FOR FURTHER RESEARCH

The concept of a "care continuum" provides a better way of measuring and valuing child care than a simple distinction between primary and secondary care. The ATUS provides an invaluable tool for exploring supervisory and both indirect and direct activities of care. But this tool needs to be sharpened carefully before moving toward efforts to assign a value to unpaid child care as a whole. While some aspects of supervisory care are omitted (such as time that children are sleeping at night), the intensity of supervisory care may be relatively low. We believe that the highest priority for further research is the analysis of the density of care (ratio of adults to children) and its implications for care quality. Other determinants of quality also require concerted interdisciplinary attention.

Probably the most important message of this chapter is that efforts to assign a market value to nonmarket work in the United States should not rely simply on measures of time devoted to housework, household management, and child care. Supervisory child care is quantitatively and qualitatively significant, and the constraints that it imposes on adults' activities are crucial to any analysis of the interaction between the market and nonmarket sectors of the economy.

Appendix 2A
Detailed ATUS Codes
Corresponding to Table 2.2

1. Supervisory Care

The total amount of in-your-care minus the time overlapped with the following activities:

0201 housework
0202 food and drink preparation
0209 household management
07 consumer purchases
0801 child care services
0901 household services (not done for self)
160103 telephone calls to/from education services providers
160107 telephone calls to/from paid child or adult care providers
030109 cooking after household children
030199 caring for and helping household children, n.e.c.

These are duplicated for nonhousehold children.

2. Housework and Household Management Related to Children

2a. Housework

0201 housework
0202 food and drink preparation, presentation, and clean-up

2b. Household Management

0209 household management
07 consumer purchases
0801 child care services
0901 household services (not done for self)

The following activities if child is not present:

030110 attending household children's event
030202 meeting and school conference
030203 home schooling of household children

030204 waiting associated with household children's education
030299 activities related to household child's education, n.e.c.
030301 providing medical care to household children
030302 obtaining medical care for household children
030303 waiting associated with household children's health
030399 activities related to household child's health, n.e.c.
030108 organizing and planning for household children
030111 waiting for/with household children
030112 picking up/dropping off household children
170301 care-related travel for household child

These are duplicated for nonhousehold children.

160103 telephone calls to/from education services providers
160107 telephone calls to/from paid child or adult care providers

3. Direct Care

3a. Physical Care

030101 physical care for household children
040101 physical care for nonhousehold children

The following activities if child is present:

030301 providing medical care to household children
030302 obtaining medical care for household children
030303 waiting associated with household children's health
030399 activities related to household child's health, n.e.c.
030111 waiting for/with household children
030112 picking up/dropping off household children
170301 care-related travel for household child

These are duplicated for nonhousehold children.

3b. Developmental Care

030201 homework
030102 reading to/with household children
030103 playing with household children, not sports
030104 arts and crafts with household children
030105 playing sports with household children
030106 talking with/listening to household children
030107 helping/teaching household children (not related to education)

These are duplicated for nonhousehold children.

The following activities if child is present:

030108 organizing and planning for household children
030110 attending household children's event
030202 meeting and school conference
030203 home schooling of household children
030204 waiting associated with household children's education
030299 activities related to household child's education, n.e.c.

These are duplicated for nonhousehold children.

Notes

1. A replacement wage estimate is based on what it would cost to hire someone to do comparable work. The NAS report recommends a replacement cost approach rather than an opportunity cost approach based on what the person performing the work potentially could have earned.

2. An example of a child-centric survey is the Child Development Supplement of the Panel Study of Income Dynamics (CDS-PSID), which is analyzed in Folbre et al. (2005). Some estimates of the value of adult time received by children are provided in Folbre (2008).

3. The Swedish per-child family allowance, according to laws implemented in 1999, came to 950 Kronor per child per month. At the exchange rate of $1 = 7.31 kronor, this comes to $1,559.50 per year per child (U.S. Social Security Administration 2004). For level of U.S. tax benefits see later discussion, especially Table 2.1.

4. This represents a weighted average of weekdays, Saturdays, and Sundays. Note also that "in your care" time, as defined by the ATUS, excludes time that an adult was engaged in an activity of child care. The two categories are nonoverlapping.

5. Adults living in households with children over the age of 12 are excluded because primary activities of child care could be devoted to these children but "in your care" could not be.

6. In a previous presentation at the American Time Use Early Results Conference in Bethesda, Maryland, in December 2005, we provided a somewhat different characterization of the care continuum, dividing it into two parts, direct and indirect care.

7. A nonlinear transformation of the density of care, such as the square root of the child-adult ratio, could provide a reasonable way of weighting inputs of time, paralleling the economies-of-scale parameters applied in household equivalence scales. But the relationship between density and care inputs probably varies with social context and age of children.

8. International Nanny Association, INA Nanny Salary and Benefits Survey, available on line at http://www.nanny.org/INA_Salary_Survey2.pdf, accessed December 30, 2005.

References

Abraham, Katherine, and Christopher Mackie, eds. 2004. *Beyond the Market. Designing Nonmarket Accounts for the United States*. Washington, DC: The National Academies Press.

Battle, Ken, and Michael Mendelson, eds. 2001. *Benefits for Children: A Four Country Study*. Ottawa: The Caledon Institute.

Bittman, Michael, and Judy Wajcman. 2004. "The Rush Hour: The Quality of Leisure Time and Gender Equity." In *Family Time, The Social Organization of Care*, Nancy Folbre and Michael Bittman, eds. New York: Routledge, pp. 171–194.

Bojer, Hilde, and Julie Nelson. 1999. "Equivalence Scales and the Welfare of Children: A Comment on, 'Is There Bias in the Economic Literature on Equivalence Scales?'" *Review of Income and Wealth* 45(4): 531–534.

Brooks-Gunn, J., W-J. Han, and J. Waldfogel. 2002. "Maternal Employment and Child Cognitive Outcomes in the First Three Years of Life: The NICHD Study of Early Child Care." *Child Development* 73: 1052–1072.

Budig, Michelle, and Paula England. 2001. "The Wage Penalty for Motherhood." *American Sociological Review* 66(2): 204–225.

Budig, Michelle, and Nancy Folbre. 2004. "Activity, Proximity, or Responsibility? Measuring Parental Childcare Time." In *Family Time: The Social Organization of Care*. Routledge IAFFE Advances in Feminist Economics, 2. London: Routledge, pp. 51–68.

Calhoun, Charles A., and Thomas J. Espenshade. 1988. "Childbearing and Wives' Foregone Earnings." *Population Studies* 42(1): 5–37.

Craig, Lyn. 2005. "The Effect of Children on Adults' Time-Use: An Analysis of the Incremental Time Costs of Children in Australia." Social Policy Research Center Discussion Paper no.143. Sydney, Australia: Social Policy Research Centre, University of New South Wales.

Ferreira, M. Luisa, Reuben C. Buse, and Jan-Paul Chavas. 1998. "Is There a Bias in Computing Household Equivalence Scales?" *Review of Income and Wealth* 44(2): 183–198.

Folbre, Nancy. 2008. *Valuing Children. Rethinking the Economics of the Family*. Cambridge, MA: Harvard University Press.

Folbre, Nancy, and Jayoung Yoon. 2007. "What Is Child Care? Lessons from Time-Use Surveys of English-Speaking Countries." *Review of Economics of the Household* 5(3): 223–248.

Folbre, Nancy, Jayoung Yoon, Kade Finnoff, Alison Fuligni. 2005. "By What Measure? Family Time Devoted to Children in the United States." *Demography* 42(2): 373–390.

Frazis, Harley, and Jay Stewart. 2004. "Where Does the Time Go? Concepts and Measurement in the American Time Use Survey." In *Hard-to-Measure Goods and Services: Essays in Memory of Zvi Griliches*, Ernst Berndt and Charles Hulten, eds. National Bureau of Economic Research Studies in Income and Wealth, University of Chicago Press, pp. 73–98.

Freeman, Richard B., and Schettkat, Ronald. 2005. "Marketization of Household Production and the EU-US Gap in Work." *Economic Policy* 20(41): 6–50.

Grossman, Michael. 2003. "Education and Nonmarket Outcomes." Draft prepared for *Handbook of the Economics of Education*, Erik Hanushek and Finis Welch, eds., May. Amsterdam: North Holland, Elsevier Science.

International Nanny Association. 2004–2005. "INA Nanny Salary and Benefits Survey." http://www.nanny.org/INA_Salary_Survey2.pdf (accessed December 30, 2005).

Ironmonger, Duncan. 2004. "Bringing Up Bobby and Betty: The Inputs and Outputs of Child Care Time." In *Family Time: The Social Organization of Care*, Michael Bittman and Nancy Folbre, eds. New York: Routledge, pp. 93–109.

Joshi, Heather. 1990. "The Cash Opportunity Costs of Childbearing: An Approach to Estimation using British Data." *Population Studies* 44(1): 41–60.

Juster, F. Thomas, and Frank Stafford. 1991. "The Allocation of Time: Empirical Findings, Behavioral Models, and Problems of Measurement." *Journal of Economic Literature* 29(2): 471–522.

Kahneman, D., A.B. Krueger, S. Schkade, N. Schwarz, and A.A. Stone. 2004. "A Survey Method for Characterizing Daily Life Experience. The Day Reconstruction Method." *Science* 306(5702): 1776–1780.

Lareau, Annette. 2003. *Unequal Childhoods. Class, Race, and Family Life.* Berkeley: University of California Press.

Leibowitz, Arleen. 1973. "Home Investments in Children." In *Economics of the Family. Marriage, Children, and Human Capital*, T.W. Schultz, ed. Chicago: University of Chicago Press, pp. 432–456.

Lino, Mark. 2001a. *Expenditures on Children by Families*. 2000 Annual Report. Miscellaneous Publication no. 1528-2000. Washington, DC: U.S. Department of Agriculture, Center for Nutrition Policy and Promotion.

_____. 2001b. "USDA's Expenditures on Children by Families Project: Uses and Changes Over Time." *Family Economics and Nutrition Review* 13(1): 81–86.

Mattingly, M.J., and S. Bianchi. 2003. "Gender Differences in the Quantity and Quality of Free Time: The U.S. Experience." *Social Forces* 81(3): 999–1030.

Presser, Harriet. 1994. "Employment Schedules among Dual-Earner Spouses and the Division of Household Labor by Gender." *American Sociological Review* 59(3): 348–364.

_____. 1995. "Job, Family, and Gender: Determinants of Nonstandard Work Schedules among Employed Americans in 1991." *Demography* 32(4): 577–598.

Reid, Margaret. 1934. *The Economics of Household Production*. New York: John Riley.

Robinson, Warren. 1987. "The Time Cost of Children and Other Household Production." *Population Studies* 41(2): 313–323.

Schwartz, Lisa K. 2001. "Minding the Children: Understanding How Recall and Conceptual Interpretations Influence Responses to a Time-Use Summary Question." Unpublished paper, U.S. Bureau of Labor Statistics, Washington, DC.

U.S. Social Security Administration. 2004. *Social Security Programs through the World: Europe, 2004*. Social Security Administration, Washington, DC. http://www.ssa.gov/policy/docs/progdesc/ssptw/2004-2005/europe/sweden .html (accessed May 28, 2008).

Waldfogel, Jane. 1997. "The Effect of Children on Women's Wages." *American Sociological Review* 62(2): 209–217.

Whitebook, Marcy, and Laura Sakai. 2003. *By a Thread: How Child Care Centers Hold on to Teachers, How Teachers Build Lasting Careers*. Kalamazoo, MI: W.E. Upjohn Institute for Employment Research.

3

Does Housework Continue to Narrow the Income Gap?

The Impact of American Housework on Economic Inequality over Time

Cathleen D. Zick
University of Utah

W. Keith Bryant
Cornell University

Anyone who has ever tackled a pile of dirty laundry, contemplated what to cook for dinner, helped a child with a homework problem, or tended a garden knows that time spent doing household chores enhances a household's overall quality of life. If a member of the household does not do the chore, the services must be purchased in the market at some cost or the task goes undone and the household's quality of life suffers. For example, if someone does not cook dinner, the alternatives are to purchase a prepared meal (at a full-service or fast-food restaurant) or snack on leftovers that require no preparation. Purchasing a prepared meal takes money that might be better spent on other things, and snacking on leftovers may not be desirable for aesthetic or health reasons (depending on how long the leftovers have been in the refrigerator). Thus, on many evenings, people devote time and energy to preparing their dinners.

Virtually all Americans dedicate some time and energy to housework with the aim of augmenting their quality of life. Data from the 2005 American Time Use Survey (ATUS) reveal that women age 15 and older devote an average of 28 hours per week to household chores, while men age 15 and older devote 16.1 hours. Housekeeping, meal preparation and cleanup, shopping, and physical and nonphysical care of household members are the subcategories where women and men allocate the largest amounts of time. For women the average amount of time devoted to all household chores exceeds the average amount of time they devote to paid employment in a typical week, and for men it is slightly less than half the amount of time they spend in paid employment in an average week (U.S. Bureau of Labor Statistics 2006).

Despite the large amounts of time devoted to household chores, social scientists took little note of its economic importance until the 1960s and 1970s, when simplistic labor-leisure models of time allocation were expanded to incorporate unpaid productive activities in the home (Becker 1965; Gronau 1977). Today, there is no doubt among social scientists that the time spent cooking meals, laundering clothing, gardening, caring for children, and so forth, enhances both economic and social-psychological well-being (Becker 1991; Bianchi, Robinson, and Milkie 2006; Bryant and Zick 2006; Folbre and Bittman 2004; Hochschild 1989).

Recognition of the economic importance of household chores has led to an international literature seeking to incorporate housework and other nonmarket work (such as volunteer work) into a system of national accounts that document the economic activities of countries (see, for example, Ironmonger [1996]; Landefeld, Fraumeni, and Vojtech [2005]; Landefeld and McCulla [2000]; and Lutzel [1996]). At the same time, a much smaller literature has arisen that asks whether housework, when valued monetarily and added to household income, markedly changes the distribution of economic well-being within a society. If low-income households do more housework than high-income households, and if the per hour value of low-income households' housework is similar to that done by high-income households, then housework makes the distribution of economic well-being more equal. If, on the other hand, low-income households do less housework than more affluent households and/or if the per hour value of housework is positively correlated with money income, then household chores may well exacerbate income inequality.

Does housework worsen or ameliorate income inequalities? Prior research that makes use of data from time diary surveys to address this question is limited to three studies. Research by Frazis and Stewart

(2006) using the ATUS data reveals that in the United States, including the value of household work in a more encompassing measure of income reduces income inequality by roughly 20 percent in 2003. The two other diary-based studies have been done using data from Denmark (Bonke 1992) and Norway (Aslaksen and Koren 1996). These are countries with much lower levels of income inequality than in the United States, yet the authors of these two studies also conclude that the monetary value of housework reduces income inequality by 10–30 percent.

Has housework always served as a moderate equalizing force within American society? Has its impact varied over time? Was housework a more potent force in earlier times, when the fraction of households headed by married couples was larger and it was more likely that the wife was a full-time homemaker with minor children in the home? Or, has its importance for economic well-being grown over time as Americans' incomes have grown more unequal?

SOCIODEMOGRAPHIC CHANGE

There have been profound sociodemographic changes over the past quarter century, many of which are intertwined with one another. While it is clearly beyond the scope of this chapter to disentangle the causal links among these phenomena, it is important to provide an overview of these simultaneous trends so that we have the appropriate context for assessing how housework time has shifted and what the shift implies for the distribution of economic well-being in the United States. Toward that end, we briefly describe six interrelated phenomena: the rise of diverse household types, the increases in women's educational levels and labor force participation rates, the decline in fertility rates, the changing racial/ethnic mix, and the aging of the population.

U.S. census data show that in 1970, 69.4 percent of all households in the United States were married couple households. By 2000, this number had dropped to 51.7 percent. At the same time all other household types grew: other family households (e.g., single parents) increased from 10.9 percent to 16.4 percent, one-person households rose from 17.6 percent to 25.8 percent, and nonfamily households (e.g., roommates) went from 2.1 percent to 6.1 percent (Hobbs and Stoops 2002). In terms of our living arrangements, America essentially became a more demographically heterogeneous nation over this period.

In 1970, 1 in 7 American males and 1 in 12 American females had completed four or more years of college. Over the next 35 years, the educational attainment of American men and women grew precipitously, with the rate of gain for women being slightly larger than for men. By 2005, 26.5 percent of American women had completed four or more years of college while 28.9 percent of American men achieved this benchmark (U.S. Census Bureau 2007, Table A-2).

As American women's educational levels rose, so too did their labor force participation rates. In 1970, 43.3 percent of all women aged 16 and older were employed outside of the home. By 2000, this number had increased to 59.5 percent (U.S. Bureau of the Census 2007, Table 575). Perhaps even more noteworthy is the fact that the growth in the labor force participation rates of married women with one or more children under age six—typically the group that spends the most time doing household chores—outpaced the growth in the overall labor force participation rates for American women. Between 1975 and 2003, the employment rates of married mothers with children under age six grew from 36.7 percent to 59.8 percent (U.S. Census Bureau 2007, Table 585).

While women's education levels and labor force participation rates were rising, American fertility rates were moving in the opposite direction. In 1976, the average number of children ever born to women aged 40–44 was 3.09. By 2004, the number had plummeted to 1.90. The drop in fertility was slightly larger for ever-married women, but the overall decline was offset somewhat by an increase in children born to never-married women (U.S. Census Bureau 2007, Table H2).

Interwoven with changes in Americans' household composition, educational attainment, and labor supply has been a trend toward greater racial/ethnic diversity. In 1970, 87.5 percent of Americans were white, 11.1 percent were black, and 1.4 percent were of other races. By the 2000 census, only 75.1 percent of Americans were white, 12.3 percent were black, and 12.5 percent were of other races. Simultaneously, between the 1980 and 2000 censuses, the Hispanic population in the United States climbed from 6.4 percent to 12.5 percent (Hobbs and Stoops 2002, Figures 3-3 and 3-5).

Finally, the American population has grown older over the past several decades. In 1970, the median age in the United States was 28.1. By 2000, it had risen to 35.3 (Hobbs and Stoops 2002, Figure 2-5). This substantial increase in the median age reflects the aging of the relatively large baby boom generation and the relatively smaller baby bust generation that has followed.

IMPLICATIONS OF SOCIODEMOGRAPHIC CHANGE FOR HOUSEHOLD INCOME

The sociodemographic trends described above, along with alterations in labor markets, have triggered changes in household income over the past 40 years. For instance, in households headed by married couples with minor children present, the increase in women's labor force participation rates has been a contributing factor to the growth in median household income. Real median household income for the married-couple households grew by 25.3 percent between 1969 and 1996 (McNeil 1998). Yet, for much of this time span, married males' real earnings remained relatively constant. By sending a second earner into the labor market, these families were able to improve their monetary standard of living. Indeed, when the earnings of wives are excluded from the calculation of the change in median income over this period, the real growth rate for married couples with minor children is only 1.5 percent (McNeil 1998).

At the same time, the proliferation of racially and demographically diverse household types, coupled with growing earnings disparities by education level, has precipitated an increase in money income inequality. Households headed by single individuals typically have lower incomes than households headed by married couples. Similarly, households headed by racial minorities typically have lower incomes than households headed by whites. Both the growing diversity of household types and the greater racial and ethnic heterogeneity have contributed to the increase in household income inequality. Analysis of income data from the current population survey reveal that income inequality increased by 25 percent between 1970 and 2003 (DeNavas-Walt, Proctor, and Lee 2006).

IMPLICATIONS OF SOCIODEMOGRAPHIC CHANGE FOR HOUSEWORK

What have these sociodemographic changes wrought for the time Americans spend doing household chores? Lower fertility rates reduce the demand for housework, especially child care. As more women have earned college degrees and entered the paid labor market, the opportunity costs of doing housework have also increased. This has likely led to the substitution of some male time for female time spent doing household chores. Simultaneously, these forces have also likely encouraged households to substitute capital for labor in the home by adopting new, labor-saving household technologies (such as dishwashers) and purchasing substitute services in the marketplace (such as lawn care services).

Analyses of time diary data collected in surveys done periodically over the past four decades reveal that married women's housework time has declined while the housework time of married men rose over this same period. The average housework time of single individuals has always been less than that of their married counterparts. Thus, the decline in housework time for all adult females has been even sharper, and the growth for all adult males has been more modest because of the simultaneous increase in nonmarried households over this period. For example, Sayer's (2005) analysis of historical time diary data reveals that the typical American mother spent about 4.5 hours per day in housework in 1965. By 1998 this average had declined to 2.7 hours per day. The comparable figures for all women (i.e., mothers and nonmothers) was 4.0 hours per day in 1965 and 2.2 hours per day in 1998. Fathers in 1965 averaged 38 minutes per day in household chores, but by 1998 their average climbed to 1.7 hours per day. When looking at all adult males, the increase is slightly more modest, however, changing from 37 minutes per day in 1965 to 1,6 hours per day in 1998.

Has the reduction in housework been strictly a phenomenon experienced by the rich? If so, then the reduction in housework would serve to offset the growing dispersion in income. But, if the decline in housework was unrelated to household income, or if it was disproportionately a phenomenon experienced by poor households, then it would serve to widen the economic gap between the rich and the poor.

MEASURING HOUSEWORK IN 1975 AND 2003

We use data from two nationally representative time diary surveys to assess changes in the impact of housework on income inequality in the United States. The first survey, *Time Use in Economic and Social Accounts, 1975–1976* (TUESA) (Juster et al. 2001), gathered 24-hour diary data on a random sample of 1,519 adults aged 18 or older and the 887 spouses of the respondents who were married. The respondents and their spouses were interviewed on four separate occasions, and during each interview they were asked a number of questions about their living arrangements, employment, and so forth. In addition, at the time of each interview, they completed a 24-hour time diary. The TUESA data set is the earliest, nationally representative U.S. time diary data collection effort. The TUESA sample used in the analyses that follow includes the 1,484 households that provided time diary information.

The second data set used in the analyses is the *2003 American Time Use Survey* (ATUS) (U.S. Bureau of Labor Statistics 2006) described in the introductory chapter in this volume. In order to obtain detailed income data, we restrict our ATUS sample to those respondents who participated in the 2003 March supplement to the Current Population Survey. Approximately one-third of the sample can be linked to the March supplement. We also exclude ATUS respondents aged 15–17 and respondents over age 18 who reside with their parents, in order to maximize comparability between the TUESA and ATUS samples. The ATUS gathers a single time diary for one randomly selected respondent in the household. We used these reports to generate estimates of housework time for both respondents and their spouses. The estimates for both are generated from multiple regression equations that include known sociodemographic and economic characteristics of the respondent and the spouse. The final sample size for the ATUS in the analyses that follow is 5,534 households. Further details on the construction of the TUESA and ATUS samples are available in Zick, Bryant, and Srisukhumbowornchai (2007).

In both data sets, we define housework to include reports of time spent doing interior housework; laundry and textile repair; food and drink preparation, presentation, and clean-up; interior and exterior maintenance; maintenance of lawn, garden, and houseplants; animal and pet care; vehicle maintenance; appliance and tools maintenance; household management; caring for family members; and shopping. This measure is consistent with the criteria typically used by economists to measure housework in that it includes all activities that could have been purchased in the marketplace if a household member had not spent time doing them (for example, individuals can make their own dinner or pay someone else to prepare a meal).

In the case of the ATUS, daily time spent in household activities based on the diary reports is estimated using multivariate regressions undertaken separately by marital status and gender. From these regressions, predicted housework times are generated, adjusted for day of the week (i.e., weekend versus weekday), and then converted to estimates of annual hours of housework. For the TUESA data, weekly time spent in housework is estimated based on a similar regression approach. The predicted values are multiplied by 52 to get annual hours of housework.

We use a replacement cost approach to derive an economic value for each hour spent doing household chores.[1] That is, we assess what it would cost to hire someone to do the housework if it was not done by a household member.[2] Our replacement cost estimates of the hourly value of housework are derived from multiple regressions where the hourly wage rate for housekeepers is regressed on region of residence and urban/rural location to adjust for local differences in housekeepers' wage rates. Data from the annual March supplements to the Current Population Survey are used in these estimating equations. Specifically, we restrict the 2003 March supplement to those respondents who identified their primary occupations as "maid/housekeeper," while the 1976 March supplement sample is restricted to those respondents who identified "private household workers" as their primary occupation.[3]

The wage regression coefficients are used to generate predicted replacement wages for household members in the ATUS and TUESA based on region of residence and urban/rural location. In the 1975 TUE-SA, the hourly replacement wage varies from a low of $3.27/hr. for households living in the rural west to $4.62/hr. for households living in the urban northeast (measured in 2002 dollars). In contrast, the lowest replacement wage in the 2003 ATUS is $6.33/hr. in the rural south, and the highest replacement wage is $8.00/hr. in the urban northeast (measured in 2002 dollars).

To obtain an estimate of the economic value of housework, we multiply the hourly value of housework by estimates of the annual time spent in housework for each adult in the household. These figures are then summed across adults in the household to arrive at an overall measure of the economic value of housework done in each household during the year.

Annual household income figures for the ATUS sample are drawn from the March supplement to the Current Population Survey. Annual household income figures for the TUESA sample are taken directly from the TUESA survey. These latter figures are inflated to 2003 dollars using the Personal Consumption Expenditure Deflator (Federal Reserve Bank of St. Louis 2007). Both income measures are adjusted for federal income taxes so that they reflect the household's after-tax access to purchased goods and services in the marketplace. All of the analyses that follow have been weighted using the recommended sampling weights so that the results can be generalized to the larger U.S. population as it was constituted in 1975 and 2003.

THE DISTRIBUTION OF INCOME AND HOUSEWORK IN 1975 AND 2003

The mean values for annual hours of housework in each year by gender and marital status appear in Table 3.1. These figures confirm the general trends in women's and men's housework reported in other diary-based studies (Bianchi, Robinson, and Milkie 2006; Sayer 2005). In 1975, married women averaged 36 hours per week in housework, fol-

Table 3.1 Mean Hours per Year Spent in Housework: 1975 and 2003

	1975	2003	Percentage change
Single women	1,297	1,156	−10.9
Single men	630	712	13.0
Married women	1,874	1,789	−4.5
Married men	735	1,046	42.0

SOURCE: Authors' calculations.

lowed by single women at 25 hours per week, married men at 14 hours per week, and single men at 12 hours per week. By 2003, both married and single women's average time spent in housework had declined by about three hours per week. In contrast, single men's housework time had increased by almost two hours per week, and married men's time had increased by almost six hours per week.

One strategy for summarizing income inequality is to rank households from the very poorest to the very richest and then selectively compare incomes at various percentiles. Table 3.2 shows the distributions of annual income, the estimated replacement value of housework time, and the sum of income plus the replacement value of housework (i.e., what we call extended income) in 1975 and 2003 at the 90th, 50th, and 10th percentiles. By making comparisons between these percentiles, we provide a picture of the distribution of economic well-being while avoiding the extreme values that may be subject to serious reporting error.

The first panel of Table 3.2 illustrates the growth in income inequality between 1975 and 2003. Across the two surveys, real income for the 10th percentile grew by only 29 percent, while for the 90th percentile it grew by 75 percent. The second panel also reveals growth in the inequality of housework over this era: those at the 10th percentile increased their housework by 88 percent and those at the 90th percentile increased their value of housework by 118 percent. However, the households whose members are doing little housework may be rich or poor from a monetary perspective. Thus, to get the complete picture, we need to look at the last panel where extended income—that is, the sum of income and the value of housework—has been ranked. Here we see that while there have been economic gains over time across the extended income distribution, these gains have been relatively greater

Table 3.2 Distribution of the Components of Extended Income: 1975 and 2003

	1975[a]	2002–03	Percentage change from 1975 to 2002–03
After-tax income			
10th Percentile	9,275	11,928	29
50th Percentile	28,548	40,100	41
90th Percentile	54,307	94,993	75
Mean	31,891	50,357	58
Value of housework			
10th Percentile	2,924	5,508	88
50th Percentile	7,818	17,509	124
90th Percentile	11,489	25,017	118
Mean	7,391	16,027	117
Extended income (i.e., income + value of housework)			
10th Percentile	14,314	21,504	50
50th Percentile	36,122	56,745	57
90th Percentile	64,988	115,597	78
Mean	39,312	66,384	69

[a] All 1975–1976 dollar figures have been inflated to 2002 dollars using the Personal Consumption Expenditure Deflator (Federal Reserve Bank of St. Louis 2007).
SOURCE: Authors' calculations.

for those at the higher end of the distribution. Specifically, those in the 90th percentile experienced an 80 percent increase in extended income, while those households at the 10th percentile experienced only a 50 percent increase.

Another way to assess the change is to look at how the economic value of housework changed for households in the bottom 10 percent of the money income distribution compared to how it changed for households in the top 10 percent. Our calculations (not shown in Table 3.2) reveal that the median economic value of housework increased by 30 percent over this 28-year period for those in the bottom decile of the after-tax income distribution. In contrast, the median value of housework rose by 100 percent for those in the top after-tax income decile. The bottom line is that overall economic inequality grew over this period because both after-tax income and the economic value of housework became more unequally distributed.

THE IMPACT OF SOCIODEMOGRAPHIC CHANGE ON ECONOMIC INEQUALITY

Over the years spanned by the two surveys, Americans' sociodemographic characteristics changed substantially. As noted earlier, by 2003, Americans were older, less likely to be white-non-hispanic, less likely to married/cohabitating, and had fewer children than in 1975. In addition, women were more highly educated and more likely to be employed outside of the home. Have shifts in the sociodemographic composition of the population exacerbated or ameliorated the changes in economic inequality in extended income that we observe between 1975 and 2003?

To assess the impact of the sociodemographic shifts in the population, we undertake a counterfactual analysis. To do this, we impose the sociodemographic structure of the 1975 sample on the 2003 sample. For instance, this means that we place an increased emphasis on those households where the wife was not employed in 2003 while deemphasizing those households where the wife was employed. This is done by making adjustments to the sample weights so that the sociodemographic picture portrayed in the 2003 ATUS mirrors the sociodemographic characteristics of the 1975 TUESA sample.

Figure 3.1 shows the distribution of income in 1975 and 2003. It also shows the 2003 counterfactual distribution; that is, it shows what the distribution of income would have looked like in 2003 had there been no sociodemographic change between 1975 and 2003. Comparison of the 2003 counterfactual distribution with the actual 2003 distribution reveals that if the sociodemographic characteristics of the population had not changed, income would have been lower at the 90th, 50th, and 10th percentiles.

Comparisons between the 1975 income distribution and the counterfactual 2003 income distribution show how much economic well-

Figure 3.1 Decomposition of the Change in Income Distribution: 1975–2003 ($ per year)

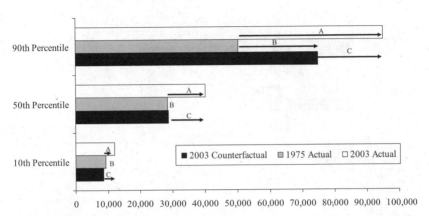

NOTE: A is overall change. B is residual change. C is change due to demographics.
SOURCE: Authors' calculations.

being changed for reasons other than sociodemographic shifts. These comparisons hold the sociodemographic composition of the two samples constant. As such, they measure the "residual" change attributable to factors other than sociodemographic trends. These changes could be the result of such things as advances in household technology, shifts in the demand for paid and unpaid labor, and the impact of ever-evolving social norms with regard to paid employment, housework, and leisure. Figure 3.1 reveals that these combined effects were very small in the middle and the lower tail of the distribution. However, at the upper end (i.e., the 90th percentile), they served to increase income substantially.

Figure 3.2 presents the decomposition of the change in extended income between 1975 and 2003. The pattern that emerges is quite similar to the one presented in Figure 3.1. Comparisons of the 2003 counterfactual extended income distribution to the actual 2003 income distribution reveal that sociodemographic shifts in the population were responsible for much of the growth in extended income that occurred over this period. Holding sociodemographics constant (i.e., comparing the 2003 counterfactual bars to the 1975 actual bars), we see that other forces had only modest impact except, again, at the very high end of

**Figure 3.2 Decomposition of the Change in Income Plus Housework
Distribution: 1975–2003 ($ per year)**

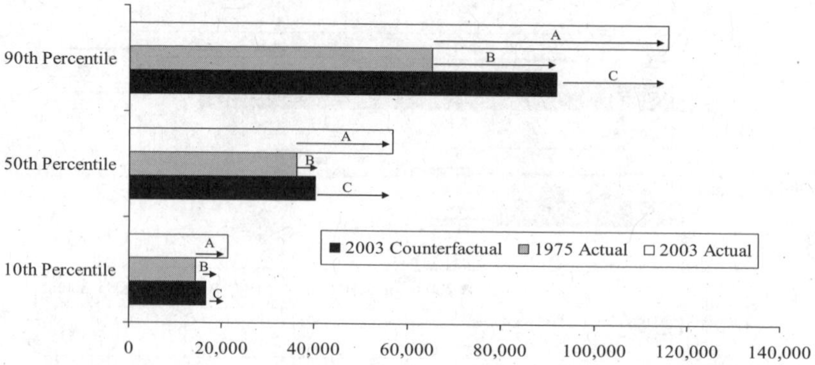

NOTE: A is overall change. B is residual change. C is change due to demographics.
SOURCE: Authors' calculations.

the distribution. The net effect (i.e., comparing 1975 actual with 2003 actual) was that extended income grew more at the 90th percentile than it did at the 10th percentile, thus increasing economic inequality over this time period.

The growth in economic inequality is depicted in Figure 3.3. The bottom bar on the graph represents the gap between high- and low-income households in 1975, while the third bar from the bottom represents the same comparison in 2003. The figure shows that the increase in income inequality over this period is primarily attributable to the relatively greater increase in after-tax income experienced by those at the top end of the income distribution. That is, "the rich got richer" compared to the average household while the poor's position changed little relative to the average.

In both 1975 and 2003, the addition of the value of housework to income to form extended income (second bar from the bottom and third bar from the top) reduces economic inequality. The reduction in economic inequality in absolute terms is greater in 1975 than in 2003. But, in relative terms, the reductions are almost identical. For example, look at the change in the ratio of the 90th percentile to the 10th percentile of extended income in each of the years. For 1975, the addition of house-

Figure 3.3 Relative Economic Well-Being as Measured by Income Plus the Value of Housework in 1975 and 2003

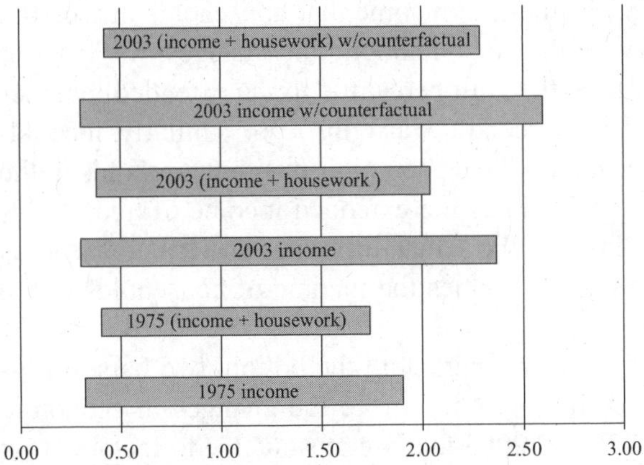

	P10/P50 Low income	P90/P50 High income	P90/P10 Decile ratio
2003 (income + housework) w/counterfactual	0.42	2.29	5.50
2003 income w/counterfactual	0.30	2.60	8.72
2003 (income + housework)	0.38	2.04	5.38
2003 income	0.30	2.37	7.96
1975 (income + housework)	0.40	1.74	4.40
1975 income	0.32	1.90	5.86

0.00 0.50 1.00 1.50 2.00 2.50 3.00

NOTE: Length of bars represents the gap between high- and low-income households. For example, in 1975, those in the 10th percentile have only 32 percent of the median income while those in the 90th percentile have 190 percent of the median income. Numbers in the first two columns of the table are the fraction of median household income. Numbers in the last column of the table represent the 90th percentile income as a fraction of the 10th percentile income.
SOURCE: Authors' calculations.

work reduces this ratio by 34 percent (5.83 to 4.40). Similarly, in 2003, the ratio of the 90th percentile to the 10th percentile is reduced by 32 percent when the value of housework is added to income. Thus, when comparing 1975 and 2003, Figure 3.3 shows that the income equalizing effects of housework are substantial and relatively similar in percentage terms in each of these years.

The two uppermost panels in Figure 3.3 depict relative economic well-being for the 2003 ATUS sample standardized to the sociodemographic profile present in the 1975 TUESA sample. They show what relative economic inequality would have looked like in the 2003 sample if the sociodemographic composition in 1975 had remained unchanged through 2003. This diagram shows clearly that both income and extended income would have grown even more unequal if the American population had not concurrently experienced considerable sociodemographic change. Again, this is especially true for the high end of the income distribution.

Without sociodemographic change, households in the 90th percentile would have had 8.72 times the income that households in the 10th percentile had. But, with the sociodemographic changes, the ratio of incomes for households in the 90th percentile to the extended incomes of households in the 10th percentile was only 7.96. Similarly, inequality in extended income would have been higher with households in the 90th percentile having 5.50 times the extended income of households in the 10th percentile. Instead, the actual difference was that households in the 90th percentile had 5.38 times the income of households in the 10th percentile.

Comparisons of the top two bars with the bottom two bars in Figure 3.3 are also useful. It allows us to see the changes in economic inequality between 1975 and 2003 that are attributable to factors other than shifting sociodemographics (i.e., the residual change). Figure 3.3 reveals that one or more of these residual factors precipitated growth in economic inequality between 1975 and 2003 by disproportionately increasing extended income at the upper end of the distribution.

DISCUSSION AND CONCLUSION

Does household work reduce the economic gap between the rich and the poor in 2003 to the same degree it did in 1975? Our analyses suggest that housework serves to reduce economic inequality in the United States in 1975 and 2003. In 1975, the economic distance between the 10th and 90th percentiles shrinks by about 25 percent when the economic value of housework is added to income. In 2003, the decline in the distance between the 10th and 90th percentiles is 32 percent. Both of these figures are in keeping with the findings of the three prior studies that have been done on this topic (Aslaksan and Koren 1996; Bonke 1992; Frazis and Stewart 2006). We conclude that unpaid work performed in the home for the benefit of household members continues to be a substantial force in reducing economic inequality in 2003 despite the shifts in housework time and changes in the larger economy that have occurred over the past quarter century.

Although housework continues to serve as a partially equalizing economic force, the income inequality plus the value of housework (i.e., extended income) grew between 1975 and 2003. The P90/P10 ratio of extended income grew by a little more than 22 percent between the two surveys when looking at income plus housework. We find that this growth in economic inequality would have been moderately greater (25 percent) if there had not been concurrent shifts in marital status, age, race/ethnicity, number of children, women's education, and women's employment.

When we investigated the impact of the sociodemographic shifts one by one (not shown in the figures), we find that declines in marriage and fertility coupled with growing racial diversity served to increase income inequality between 1975 and 2003. In contrast, increases in women's education levels and labor force participation rates coupled with the general aging of the population served to reduce income inequality. On balance, these latter sociodemographic effects outweighed the former. We also find that the more modest growth in housework inequality is fueled in part by shifts in women's education and employment and by the decline in married couple households. Interestingly, the decline in the fertility rate served to reduce housework inequality over this time period.

Our analyses suggest that changes in women's educational attainment and labor market behaviors have been particularly important in raising the average income level and slowing the growth in income inequality between 1975 and 2003. As more women have entered the labor market, they have, however, cut back on housework. The time trade-off, however, has not been one-for-one. Moreover, married men have concurrently increased their housework and thus partially compensated for the reduction in their wives' housework time. While the employment and education-induced reductions in women's housework have precipitated modest growth in housework inequality between 1975 and 2003, the growth would have been even greater had it not been for the concurrent increase in married men's housework.

Controlling for changes in the sociodemographic composition of the samples, we find substantial growth in economic inequality when comparing 1975 to 2003. This rise in economic inequality appears to be a function of modest growth in the inequality of housework coupled with more sizeable growth in income inequality, particularly at the high end of the income distribution.

What factors are likely contributing to the growth in housework and income inequality, holding sociodemographic characteristics constant? We speculate that three forces may be at work. First, there have been significant labor market shifts over this historical period. Technological changes in the job skills required increased the demand for highly educated individuals who also typically command high wage rates. The demand for less-educated individuals concurrently declined as manufacturers increasingly turned to international labor markets to fulfill their unskilled labor needs. Higher wage rates for highly educated individuals are likely to raise income while simultaneously reducing time spent in housework because of the rising opportunity costs that highly educated individuals face. At the other end of the spectrum, lower real wage rates for individuals with low levels of education will generally reduce income and increase time spent on housework. Such shifts should increase income inequality while at the same time producing greater equalizing effects of housework.

Second, technological change in household production may have played a significant role in changing the distribution of the economic value of housework. Economists argue that the adoption of new technologies serves to expand family choice, which is likely to lead to an increase in the demand for time spent in productive activities within the home. At the same time, if the new technology is labor saving, it will precipitate a decline in housework. But if it is money saving, it will foster an increase in housework time. On balance then, the expected impact on housework of adopting new technologies within the home is ambiguous. (See Bryant and Zick [2006] for a more detailed discussion of this point.)

Over the past few decades, Americans have experienced considerable technological change within the household. In particular, personal computers did not even exist in 1970; but by 2003, 61.8 percent of American households owned at least one personal computer and 54.7 percent of American households had a computer with Internet access (Day, Janus, and Davis 2005). Personal computers and access to the

Internet have allowed households to change the way they shop (both in terms of gathering prepurchase information as well as making actual purchases), manage their finances, etc. But this important shift in household technology has not been evenly distributed across all income levels. The most recent statistics show that 92.2 percent of American households with incomes at or above $100,000 per year have at least one computer with Internet access in the home. In contrast, among households where the annual income is less than $25,000 per year, computer ownership is only 41 percent and Internet access is 30.7 percent (Day, Janus, and Davis 2005).

The income-related differences in computer ownership and access to the Internet may have contributed to the recent growth in housework inequality. If computer ownership increases the household's demand for all goods and services (including those "produced" at home), then time spent in housework may increase. This increase in demand may offset any labor-saving aspects of computer ownership.

Finally, education-related changes in preferences for leisure or education-related changes in opportunity costs over this historical period may play a part in this story. In their recently completed longitudinal study, Aguiar and Hurst (2007) find that between 1965 and 2003, the average American's leisure time increased, but it increased more for less-educated individuals and less for highly educated individuals. Likewise, Robinson and Godbey (1997) report that between 1965 and 1985, the "free time" of high school graduates rose on average by 6.5 hours per week. In contrast, the free time of college graduates rose on average by only 1.1 hours per week and for individuals with advanced degrees free time did not change at all over this 20-year period. If this uneven shift in leisure time is partly a function of education-related changes in social mores about leisure activities or changes in educationally related opportunity costs, then this too may partially explain the widening economic gap between the rich and the poor.

In sum, our analyses show that despite the decline in women's housework time over the past quarter century, housework continues to be an important means by which households expand their access to goods and services. Households with lower incomes continue to increase their access to goods and services proportionately more by doing housework than do households with higher incomes, thus reducing economic inequality in the United States. Yet, between 1975 and 2003, economic inequality rose in the United States largely because of the growth in after-tax income inequality but also, in part, because of modest growth in housework inequality. Demographic changes over this period, principally the rise in women's paid employment and women's educational attainment, raised the economic status of the average household and somewhat inhibited the growth in economic inequality. At the same time, some combination of changes in the labor market structure, technology within the home, leisure opportunity costs, and/or leisure preferences likely fueled its growth.

Notes

1. Alternatively, some researchers have used an opportunity cost measure of time spent in housework (Bonke 1992; Bryant and Zick 1985). This involves estimating the economic value of time spent in the "next best" activity that has been foregone to do housework. Typically, this next best activity is market work. As such, an individual's market wage rate, adjusted for the respondent's marginal tax rate, is used as the opportunity cost measure of an hour of housework.
2. Here we use a general housekeeper wage, but another option would be to use a weighted average replacement cost wage. For instance, the wage rate paid to cooks could be multiplied by the average fraction of time spent cooking and added to the wage rate paid for child care multiplied by the average fraction of time spent caring for children, etc. Since it is unlikely that a household would be able to hire all of these professionals separately for such small amounts of time (e.g., a part-time cook, a part-time bookkeeper, a part-time launderer), we elect to use the more realistic housekeeper wage rate.
3. The Current Population Survey occupational label for housekeepers changed between these two years. Thus, while the names were changed, we are measuring the same occupation in both 1976 and 2003.

References

Aguiar, Mark, and Erik Hurst. 2007. "Measuring Trends in Leisure: The Allocation of Time over Five Decades." *Quarterly Journal of Economics* 122(3): 969–1006.

Aslaksen, Iulie, and Charlotte Koren. 1996. "Unpaid Household Work and the Distribution of Extended Income: The Norwegian Experience." *Feminist Economics* 2(3): 65–80.

Becker, Gary S. 1965. "A Theory of the Allocation of Time." *Economic Journal* 75(299): 493–517.

———. 1991. *A Treatise on the Family,* Enlarged ed. Cambridge, MA: Harvard University Press.

Bianchi, Suzanne M., John P. Robinson, and Melissa A. Milkie. 2006. *Changing Rhythms of American Family Life.* New York: Russell Sage Foundation.

Bonke, Jens. 1992. "Distribution of Economic Resources: Implications of Including Household Production." *Review of Income and Wealth* 38(3): 281–293.

Bryant, W. Keith, and Cathleen D. Zick. 1985. "Income Distribution Implications of Rural Household Production." *American Journal of Agricultural Economics* 65(5): 1100–1104.

———. 2006. *The Economic Organization of the Household*, 2nd ed.,New York: Cambridge University Press.

Day, Jennifer Cheeseman, Alex Janus, and Jessica Davis. 2005. "Computer and Internet Use in the United States: 2003." *Current Population Reports* P23–208, October.

DeNavas-Walt, Carmen, Bernadette D. Proctor, and Cheryl Hill Lee. 2006. "Income, Poverty, and Health Insurance Coverage in the United States: 2005." *Current Population Reports: Consumer Income*, P60–231, August.

Folbre, Nancy, and Michael Bittman, eds. 2004. *The Social Organization of Care.* New York: Routledge.

Frazis, Harley, and Jay Stewart. 2006. "How Does Household Production Affect Earnings Inequality? Evidence from the American Time Use Survey." U.S. Bureau of Labor Statistics Working Paper no. 393. Washington, DC: U.S. Bureau of Labor Statistics. http://www.bls.gov/ore/abstract/ec/ ec060050.htm (accessed November 21, 2007).

Gronau, Ruben. 1977. "Leisure, Home Production, and Work—The Theory of the Allocation of Time Revisited." *Journal of Political Economy* 85(6): 1099–1123.

Hobbs, Frank and Nicole Stoops. 2002. "Demographic Trends in the 20th Century." *Census 2000 Special Reports* CENSR-5, November.

Hochschild, Arlie. 1989. *The Second Shift: Working Parents and the Revolution at Home*. New York: Avon.

Ironmonger, Duncan. 1996. "Counting Outputs, Capital Inputs and Caring Labor: Estimating Gross Household Product." *Feminist Economics* 2(3): 37–64.

Juster, F. Thomas, Paul Courant, Greg J. Duncan, John P. Robinson, and Frank P. Stafford. 2001. *Time Use in Economic and Social Accounts, 1975–1976*. Ann Arbor, MI: Inter-University Consortium for Political and Social Research.

Landefeld, J. Steven, Barbara Fraumeni, and Cindy Vojtech. 2005. Accounting for Nonmarket Production: A Prototype Satellite Accounts Using the American Time Use Survey." U.S. Department of Commerce, Bureau of Economic Analysis Working Paper. Washington, DC: Department of Commerce. http://www.bea.gov/papers/pdf/Landefeld_Nonmarket_Production_ATUS.pdf (accessed November 21, 2007).

Landefeld, J. Steven, and Stephanie H. McCulla. 2000. "Accounting for Nonmarket Household Production within a National Accounts Framework." *Review of Income and Wealth* 46(3): 289–307.

Lutzel, Heinrich. 1996. "Household Sector Income, Consumption, and Wealth." In *The New System of National Accounts*, J.W. Kendrick, ed. Boston: Kluwer Academic Publishers, pp. 121–139.

McNeil, John. 1998. "Changes in Median Household Income: 1969 to 1996," *Current Population Reports Special Studies*, P23–196, July.

Robinson, John P., and Geoffry Godbey. 1997. *Time for Life—The Surprising Ways Americans Use Their Time*. University Park, PA: The Pennsylvania State University Press.

Sayer, Liana C. 2005. "Gender, Time and Inequality: Trends in Women's and Men's Paid Work, Unpaid Work and Free Time." *Social Forces* 84(1): 285–303.

St. Louis Federal Reserve. 2007. Personal Consumption Expenditures: Chain-type Price Index. http://research.stlouisfed.org/fred2/data/PCECTPI.txt (accessed November 21, 2007).

U.S. Bureau of Labor Statistics. 2005. *Consumer Expenditure Survey Tables*. www.bls.gov/cex/home.htm#tables.

———. 2006a. *American Time Use Survey: 2003."* http://www.bls.gov/tus/datafiles_2003.htm. (accessed November 21, 2007).

———. 2006b. "Time Use Survey—2005 Results Announced by BLS." Press Release, July 27.

U.S. Census Bureau. 2007. "The 2007 Statistical Abstract: The National Data Book." http://www.census.gov/compendia/statab/hist_stats.html (accessed November 21, 2007).

Zick, Cathleen D., W. Keith Bryant, and Sivithee Srisukhumbowornchai. 2007. "Does Housework Matter Anymore? The Shifting Impact of Housework on Economic Inequality." IPIA Working Paper no. 2006-08-09. Salt Lake City, UT: University of Utah, Institute of Public and International Affairs. http://www.ipia.utah.edu/workingpapers.html (accessed November 21, 2007).

4

Household Production, Consumption, and Retirement

Jennifer Ward-Batts
Wayne State University

There are countless studies examining retirement timing, retirement savings behavior, and consumption expenditures after retirement. We know far less about how people alter their time allocation to activities other than market work when they retire. How they alter time use upon retirement is important for several reasons. Time is allocated to both productive activities and to consumption. Without knowing how people spend time, we have an incomplete picture of both their production and consumption. By looking only at market labor supply, earnings, or expenditures, we may miss a large portion of the production or consumption we seek to measure. The fraction of production and consumption that we may be missing by not considering time allocation to activities other than market work is likely to increase substantially upon retirement. This chapter will address this shortcoming in the retirement literature by using time-diary data to examine the time allocation of individuals who are a little younger or a little older than typical retirement ages. This will provide a descriptive picture of how time allocation changes at retirement, and will contribute to the literature on the retirement consumption puzzle.

Evidence from several countries indicates that households reduce consumption expenditures substantially around the age of retirement. This pattern has been documented for the United States by Hamermesh (1984); Mariger (1987); Bernheim, Skinner, and Weinberg (2001); and Lundberg, Startz, and Stillman (2003); for Canada by Robb and Burbridge (1989); and for the United Kingdom by Banks, Blundell, and Tanner (1998).

The consumption decline appears to be widespread across consumption categories, rather than concentrated on work-related expenses, and to take the form of a discrete drop at the year of retirement. This behavior is puzzling since life-cycle consumption models predict that households will want to smooth consumption when they experience a predictable drop in income, such as at retirement. In other words, since retirement is not unexpected, households should plan for it and save sufficiently over the lifetime so that their consumption need not fall upon retirement.

After examining alternative explanations that are consistent with forward-looking life-cycle behavior, most researchers have attributed this consumption drop to myopic behavior (short-sightedness, or a lack of planning for the future) or to the systematic arrival of discouraging information at retirement. In other words, individuals are not aware of the value of their retirement benefits and assets, and more often than not are negatively surprised after retirement by this information. However, a collective model of household behavior suggests an alternative explanation: Most wives expect to live several years longer than their husbands, and therefore should prefer, absent perfect altruism, for the household to consume less as the couple ages than do husbands. Given this, and assuming that the husband's bargaining power depends upon his current income or employment status, the husband's retirement from a career job should cause deterioration in his relative influence on household decisions and therefore a decline in the couple's consumption spending.

Using Panel Study of Income Dynamics (PSID) data, Lundberg, Startz, and Stillman (2003) test this hypothesis by comparing the post-retirement consumption change of married couple households to single-person households using food consumption data from the PSID for the years 1979–1986 and 1989–1992. They find that expenditures drop at retirement by 8 to 10 percent for married couples, but do not decrease significantly for single-person households. The magnitude of the consumption drop is also found to be greater for couples with a larger age difference between spouses when the husband is older than the wife. These results lend some support to a collective rather than unitary approach to the decisions of older couples, and suggest that changes in relative bargaining power may explain at least part of the commonly observed postretirement drop in the household consumption of married couples.

Using data from several waves of the longitudinal U.S. Health and Retirement Study (HRS), Stillman and Ward-Batts (2003) find some evidence of a drop in home-prepared food expenditure after retirement in married-couple households. However, this decline in consumption is not larger in married-couple than in single-person households. Haider and Stephens (2004) show, using Retirement History Survey (RHS) and HRS data, that accounting for unexpected early retirement using sub-jective retirement expectations reduces the magnitude of the postretire-ment consumption decline by a third. They do not find evidence that the remaining decline is likely to be explained by marital bargaining. Con-sumption measures in PSID, RHS and HRS are, however, very crude. Nevertheless, evidence relating to this hypothesis is mixed.

A somewhat obvious alternate hypothesis is that household produc-tion may increase upon retirement, and that full consumption remains constant. Substituting time in home production for market-purchased goods and services might allow consumption to remain constant. Such a substitution would be rational at retirement when the opportunity cost of time falls, and so the price of home-produced goods falls relative to the price of market goods. Thus, actual consumption may remain constant while money expenditures fall. Findings of Stillman and Ward-Batts (2003) are not consistent with this hypothesis. However, as noted, con-sumption data in the HRS data are not very detailed. Further, there is a potential problem of the endogeneity of retirement, as retirement timing is endogenously chosen by the household or individual. If a household has accumulated sufficient wealth, then its members may retire earli-er than they otherwise would. If members of households with higher wealth retire, while those in lower wealth households continue working until later ages, i.e., until wealth is higher, then individuals who re-port being retired may come from systematically better off households. Therefore, we might expect to observe that retired households eat out more, for example, than households that are not retired but are of the same age.

There are various approaches to examining the hypothesis that household production increases after retirement. One is to examine richer expenditure data, looking in particular at goods that may tell us something about the degree to which household production plays a role in consumption. For example, detailed food expenditures would allow us to examine expenditures on staple foods that require more time to prepare relative to convenience foods and prepared meals (e.g., take-out or restaurant meals). This is the approach taken by Ward-Batts (2007). A second approach is to look at time allocation to various activities, and examine directly the question of whether home production time expenditures rise after retirement. That is the approach taken in this chapter. A finding that household production increases would not rule out that marital bargaining is playing a role. If there is a shift in bargaining power in favor of wives at retirement, the household may choose to spend less money on consumption, but make up for that reduced expenditure by increasing household production. Therefore, married or partnered individuals and single individuals will be analyzed separately to ascertain whether their change in time allocation before versus after retirement differs.

A third approach is to use data on both time use and expenditures by the same households to examine both time spent in household production and consumption, and money spent on market goods, including both input goods (e.g., groceries) and substitutes for home production (e.g., restaurant meals). This is the approach taken by Hamermesh (2008), who links ATUS and CPS Food Supplement Survey data for the same households to estimate a structural model of time and money expenditures on food. He finds that households that spend more money on food also spend more time on food, suggesting that money and time are not easily substitutable. However, time examined includes consumption time and production time aggregated together, whereas the current chapter will examine these separately. Hamermesh excludes people aged 65 and over in order to avoid changes in expenditures and time use at retirement. A follow-up study to the present chapter will use ATUS data linked to CPS FSS data in order to examine how both time and expenditures on food shift in the transition to retirement.

The analysis in this chapter is primarily descriptive in nature. American Time-Use Survey data from 2003 and 2004 are used to compare the time allocation of individuals at ages just before typical retirement ages to those just after typical retirement ages. Individuals are considered "preretirement" if they are under age 62, at which a sizeable fraction of individuals retire in the United States. Individuals are considered "postretirement" if they are aged 65 or older. There are large spikes in U.S. retirement at ages 62 and 65. Gustman and Steinmier (2005) show that these spikes can be explained by incentives in the Social Security system in the presence of varying rates of time preference within the population.

Age will be used as a proxy measure of retirement status, but actual labor market status will not be included in the model due to potential endogeneity bias, as mentioned above. Individual retirement timing depends on many factors. For example, households with higher wealth may retire at earlier ages than those with lower wealth. We might find that among people of a given age, the retired group eats out more and spends less time cooking. This might be due to that group having higher wealth, rather than being attributable to their retirement status. That group may have always tended to eat out more. Using actual labor market status might result in attributing differences in behavior to retirement when those differences may really be due to different characteristics of the retired versus nonretired group. So we would in effect be comparing retired apples to nonretired oranges—not the right comparison. Simply using age as a proxy for retirement status avoids this problem.

THEORETICAL BACKGROUND

Consumption

In a simple life-cycle model of consumption, individuals maximize utility—satisfaction from consumption of goods, services, and leisure—over n periods given the present discounted value of their lifetime income and the real market rate of interest. (An example of the objective function and additional technical details related to this section can be found in Appendix 4A.) How one should optimally allocate consumption over the lifetime depends both on the real interest rate and on the extent to which one cares more about consumption in some periods of life than others. Economists often simply assume that individuals care less about consumption in the future than about consumption today, and that the further in the future one looks, the less he cares about his consumption in that future period. In spite of this very simple assumption that is often made, there is a substantial literature on how the optimal level of consumption may change over the lifetime. Economists tend to focus on marginal utility, which is the additional satisfaction one gets from consuming a little more. Marginal utility decreases as total satisfaction from consumption increases. For example, we care less about having another bite when we have had lots to eat than when we have had little. Lillard and Weiss (1997) find evidence that the marginal utility from consumption rises in periods of poor health, which may imply increasing marginal utility of consumption with age in the general population, as health typically declines with age. This would suggest that the level of consumption should rise as we get older. On the other hand, we typically assume that there is a positive discount rate, so that consumption today is more highly valued than future consumption, implying decreasing marginal utility over time given constant consumption. This would suggest that total consumption should fall over the lifetime. Hyperbolic discounting is a special case of discounting future consumption. It implies time inconsistency in the rate of time preference, such that we make decisions in the present that we would want to change in the future if we could do so (Laibson 1998). For example, we might reach retirement age and then realize we'd saved too little, and wish we had saved more.

First, suppose that individuals care equally about consumption in each period of life. Then the optimal solution to the utility maximization problem implies that an individual will want to increase consumption gradually over the lifetime in the presence of a positive real interest rate. This is because the price of consumption is higher in earlier periods than in later periods, due to either paying or foregoing interest by consuming in earlier periods. However, if there is a positive rate of time preference equal to the market real interest rate, meaning that people care more about present than future consumption, then consumption should be the same in every period.

This does not imply that each element of consumption must remain constant—only that one remain indifferent between bundles of consumption in each period. One can make trade-offs by giving up some of one good and gaining more of another in order to maintain the same level of utility. A predictable change in the price of a particular good should be planned for and should not result in a discrete change in overall consumption at the time of the price change. For example, when the opportunity cost of an individual's time falls predictably, due to Social Security benefits rules, the level of satisfaction from consumption should not change. Rather, one should increase leisure consumption and decrease consumption of other goods in order to maintain a constant level of satisfaction from consumption. In other words, one should shift away from consumption of money-intensive consumption toward time-intensive consumption when the price of time falls, but the overall level of consumption, or satisfaction from that consumption, should not change.

Consumption vs. Expenditure

The above discussion is about consumption. However, what we typically measure in empirical data is expenditures. Expenditures may differ from consumption in a particular time period for several reasons. For example, durable goods are purchased in a single period but render a stream of services (consumption) over many periods. Another reason for consumption and expenditure to differ at a point in time is home production. Households use market goods and time to produce consumption goods (see Becker 1973, 1988). When the price of time allocated to household production is lower, all else constant, one should spend more time in household production. For most, the opportunity cost of time drops discretely upon retirement from a career job. Thus the price of a home-cooked meal falls at retirement relative to the price of a restaurant meal, take-out food, or a microwave dinner.

We have historically had fairly good data on expenditures on market goods purchased by households, but until recently have not had very good data on their allocation of time other than to market work. By examining only money expenditures, we miss a potentially large component of what is available to households to consume. Frazis and Stewart (2006) and Zick and Bryant (2008) show that adding the value of home production to households' income substantially reduces income inequality in the general population.

If we focus solely on income or expenditures, the missing component of consumption is arguably even more substantial after versus before retirement. By looking only at money expenditures, we therefore make biased inferences about consumption, and this bias is particularly problematic when making comparisons before versus after retirement.

DATA AND METHODS

I use the American Time Use Survey (ATUS) data described in the introduction to this volume. Pooled data from 2003 and 2004 survey years are used. Survey weights are used for all summary statistics and analyses. Men and women aged 55–61 inclusive and aged 65–71 inclusive are included in the sample. Those aged 61 and younger represent the preretirement years while those aged 65 and older represent the postretirement years. Thus, individuals up to seven years prior to age 62 and up to 7 years at and after age 65 are included. Those in the preretirement ages are compared to those after retirement ages. Labor force status and time use are jointly determined, and so labor force status will not be used as a control variable, i.e., as an explanatory variable in the regressions, as discussed at length in the first section. Examining behavior at various ages at which there are very different incentives to retire versus continue in market work that are exogenous to the individual is a less problematic approach. Time spent in market work is one of the time-use categories analyzed.

The seven-year age range encompasses a wide range of ages. We might be concerned that individuals at the younger end of this range are not comparable to those toward the end of it for several reasons. First, younger individuals may be more capable than those who are older, and thus may allocate time differently to home production and other activities for reasons unrelated to retirement. Second, younger individuals in the sample are from substantially different birth cohorts than the oldest in the sample. If there are cohort effects (i.e., generational effects) in time allocation, then this may also generate differences between the groups that are unrelated to retirement.

To address these concerns, I do two things. First, I use linear and quadratic age terms in regression analyses to pick up gradual trends in time use as people age, in addition to the postretirement-age dummy variable, which will pick up changes of a more discrete nature. Second, while the primary analysis uses seven years before and after typical retirement ages, I have also repeated these analyses using a sample that includes only three years before and after the standard retirement ages, i.e., those aged 59–61 inclusive and 65–67 inclusive. The rationale for this is that the average postretirement person in the 3-year age range is only 6 years older than the average preretirement person (66 compared to 60), while the average postretirement person in the 7-year age range sample is 10 years older than the average preretirement person (68 compared to 58). If there are systematic changes of a discrete nature as we age in how we spend time, due to changes in health, for example, then those changes may be erroneously attributed to retirement, since age is used as a proxy for retirement here. The possibility of this error may be larger in a wider sample of ages. However, when repeating the analyses with a sample including a three-year age range on either side of retirement, I find very similar patterns to those presented here.

RESULTS

Mean Difference Tests

Table 4.1 presents mean times in several types of activities for men and women in the before and after retirement groups separately. A mean difference test is performed for each activity category, and asterisks indicate statistically significant differences. Results are shown using the seven-year pre- and postretirement age sample. Results based on the seven- and three-year age ranges generally are similar in terms of means, mean differences, and levels of statistical significance.

The first five categories are household production and some of its subcategories. Housework, food preparation, maintenance and repair, and lawn and garden care are all included in aggregate home production time. Some tasks of home production are not included in these subcat-

Table 4.1 Mean Time Spent in Activities before versus after Retirement Ages

	Minutes per day			
	Women before	Women after	Men before	Men after
Home production	165.3***	207.3	103.8**	121.6
Housework	61.7***	86.9	10.7	13.5
Food prep.	58.0***	70.1	15.9**	21.5
Maintenance & repair	7.8	9.3	26.0	22.8
Lawn & garden	13.6	12.1	23.7***	36.8
Purchases & shopping	31.9	28.1	17.8***	23.9
Volunteer work	9.1	10.7	6.6**	10.9
Giving care or help	36.0	29.2	16.9	23.2
Market work	176.6***	49.5	286.2***	103.6
Travel	75.9***	60.0	71.6	67.8
Eating & drinking	70.3***	78.9	76.7***	87.3
Social & leisure	268.5***	340.7	284.5***	388.4
Sport, exercise, recreation	10.2	12.8	21.8	20.3
Religious activities	10.3	12.3	7.2***	11.9
Personal care	555.1***	578.0	530.6***	553.1

NOTE: Survey weights used. *significant at the 0.10 level; **significant at the 0.05 level; ***significant at the 0.01 level.

egories, so the aggregate category, home production, will in general be larger than their sum. Much of the time spent in purchases and shopping may also be thought of as home production of a sort but are not included in the aggregate home production time here. In postretirement relative to preretirement years, both men and women spend significantly more time in housework and food preparation, and in home production overall. Men spend more time in lawn and garden care and more time shopping and making purchases after retirement ages. Surprisingly, women spend less time shopping postretirement, but the difference is not statistically significant.

The next four categories are activities that are production of a sort other than household production, or in the case of travel, that likely are closely related to production activities. Somewhat surprisingly, men's time in volunteer work increases significantly in their postretirement years. Women's time in these activities is already fairly high in the preretirement years, relative to men, and does not appear to change when they enter postretirement ages. Women decrease time spent giving care or help to others in postretirement ages, while men increase time in such activities, although the difference is not quite significant for either. Giving care or help includes assisting both household members and nonhousehold members, and is exclusive of market work or formal volunteer work activities. Not surprisingly, both men and women decrease their time in market work activities in postretirement years. The level of time in market work is higher for men than for women in both pre- and postretirement ages, and the drop in time devoted to market work is also larger for men than for women.

Both women and men reduce travel time in postretirement-age years, but the difference is statistically significant only for women. Travel is likely to be related largely to production activities. Commute time to work, for example, should fall at retirement. Other travel time includes time spent traveling to and from shopping places, time spent taking children places, and time spent traveling to and from places where one does volunteer work. Travel time is coded according to the origination and destination of each trip, where a trip is defined as traveling between two points. If one travels from home to Starbucks, and then on from there to work, two trips are recorded. The first trip is coded as going to get coffee, and the second is coded as commuting to work. We might want to count both portions as commuting to work in this case, but it is somewhat ambiguous when we would want to recode a trip and when not. A more extensive examination of travel time is beyond the scope of this chapter.

The last five categories of activities might be thought of as largely consumption. Time spent eating and drinking and in social and leisure activities increases significantly in postretirement-age years for both men and women. Time spent in sports, exercise, and recreation increases for women, but the difference is not statistically significant. Time spent in religious activities for women does not change significantly after retirement, while men significantly increase religious activities time.[1] Both men and women increase time spent on personal care, and the difference is significant in all but the three-year age-range sample for women.

To summarize findings from mean difference tests, it appears that men and women spend more time doing almost everything except market work and travel in postretirement-age years. Interestingly, men spend more time shopping after retirement, while women decrease shopping time.

Regression Analysis

We might be concerned that the samples of individuals representing the pre- versus postretirement ages are systematically different. In other words, there may be differences between these groups in characteristics other than age, such as in education or household composition. This may result in finding differences in how they spend time that are unrelated to retirement. We can address this concern by performing multivariate regression analysis, which allows us to control for demographic factors, such as education and household composition. I do not control for income in these models, as income will be determined in part by retirement status, which I have already argued is endogenous. Educational attainment should serve as a proxy for lifetime income or earning potential.

Tables 4.2–4.5 present results from such regression models for four different samples: partnered women, single women, partnered men, and single men.[2] In all cases the broader sample of age ranges is used. Results using the narrower sample including only three years before and after retirement ages are similar and are available from the author.

For each activity category, three models are presented. First, only a constant term, a dummy variable for the year surveyed, and a dummy variable for postretirement age are included in the model. Second, controls for spouse's age and its square, own educational attainment, spouse's educational attainment, and presence of children in the household are added. Finally, own age and its square are added to the model. The latter is reserved for last since we may not expect to be able to reliably distinguish separately an age effect from a postretirement-age effect in a short age series. In interpreting results here, I generally focus on the second model for each outcome.

Partnered women (see Table 4.2) significantly increase time spent in home production in postretirement-age years, including significant increases in both housework and food preparation time. They significantly decrease time spent in market work. Time spent traveling decreases, but the difference is not significant when controls are included. Time spent socializing, relaxing, and in leisure increase, as does time spent in sport, exercise, and recreation, and time spent in personal care. This suggests that partnered women are indeed reallocating their time after retirement in ways that economic theory would predict. They are spending more time in leisure activities, and more time producing household consumption goods that are substitutes for money-intensive substitutes, such as convenience foods, restaurant meals, and maid services.

There are no statistically significant changes in home production time for single women, but they do decrease time spent in market work and travel. They increase time spent eating and drinking; socializing, relaxing, and taking leisure; doing religious activities; and in personal care. Single women (see Table 4.3) have fewer significant changes in time allocation in pre- versus postretirement years. This may be attributable in part to the substantially smaller sample size, which makes it difficult to establish statistically significant differences. At postretirement ages they spend more time eating and drinking; socializing, relaxing and taking leisure; and in personal care.

Partnered men (see Table 4.4) spend more time in home production, including time in housework and food preparation. They also spend more time shopping and less time in market work. Point estimates indicate that they spend slightly more time in volunteer work and caring for or helping others, but these increases are not statistically significant. They spend significantly more time eating and drinking; socializing, relaxing, and taking leisure; and in personal care.

There are relatively few significant results for single men (see Table 4.5). There are no statistically significant results among the various activities when using the second specification, which includes all controls except for own age. There are substantial differences in point estimates between the three specifications. This sample is quite small, and the effects are very imprecisely estimated. In the first two specifications, it appears that single men spend less time in home production at postretirement ages than at younger ages. However, when we control for his age, the point estimate becomes positive and fairly large, but not statistically significant. When age is controlled for, estimates indicate that

Table 4.2 Regression Analysis for Partnered Females (minutes per day)

A. Home production and related activities

	Home production			Housework			Food prep.			Maintenance, repair			Lawn & garden			Purchases, shopping		
Postretirement	46.8***	33.7***	29.3	26.1***	14.3*	9.5	13.6***	11.1*	12.8	2.2	-3.2	-3.6	-2.6	-2.6	-2.9	-3.5	-1.1	-10.3
	(9.1)	(12.4)	(23.1)	(6.0)	(8.2)	(17.0)	(4.4)	(6.1)	(11.2)	(2.5)	(2.9)	(7.8)	(2.4)	(2.9)	(5.4)	(3.1)	(4.2)	(7.6)
Age			-24.1			-12.2			4.4			5.8			-10.5			-1.6
			(29.1)			(19.5)			(12.3)			(8.8)			(8.1)			(8.9)
Age^2			0.2			0.1			-0.0			-0.0			0.1			0.0
			(0.2)			(0.2)			(0.1)			(0.1)			(0.1)			(0.1)
Controls?	No	Yes	Yes	No	Yes	Yes	No	Yes	Yes	No	Yes	Yes	No	Yes	Yes	No	Yes	Yes
N	1,836	1,833	1,833	1,836	1,833	1,833	1,836	1,833	1,833	1,836	1,833	1,833	1,836	1,833	1,833	1,836	1,833	1,833
R^2	0.02	0.03	0.03	0.02	0.03	0.03	0.01	0.03	0.03	0.00	0.01	0.01	0.00	0.01	0.01	0.00	0.01	0.01

B. Other production

	Volunteer work			Care for/help others			Market work			Travel		
Postretirement	2.2	4.7	4.6	-7.7	-12.6	-14.2	-124.3***	-102.3***	-11.7	-15.8***	-9.8	-8.7
	(2.5)	(3.7)	(6.8)	(5.1)	(8.3)	(14.0)	(10.9)	(16.0)	(27.3)	(4.1)	(6.0)	(10.2)
Age			5.7			8.8			-63.2*			-11.7
			(8.6)			(15.6)			(34.4)			(13.1)
Age^2			-0.0			-0.1			0.4			0.1
			(0.1)			(0.1)			(0.3)			(0.1)
Controls?	No	Yes	Yes	No	Yes	Yes	No	Yes	Yes	No	Yes	Yes
N	1,836	1,833	1,833	1,836	1,833	1,833	1,836	1,833	1,833	1,836	1,833	1,833
R^2	0.00	0.02	0.02	0.00	0.03	0.03	0.08	0.10	0.11	0.01	0.03	0.03

C. Consumption

	Eating & drinking			Socialize, relax, leisure			Sports, exercise, recreation			Religious			Personal care		
Post-retirement	7.8***	3.3	7.2	67.3***	57.2***	29.0	2.7	7.0**	3.9	1.4	-2.8	-13.1**	18.9***	17.8**	-18.0
	(2.9)	(3.9)	(8.1)	(10.6)	(14.2)	(27.2)	(2.3)	(3.4)	(6.0)	(1.9)	(2.6)	(5.5)	(6.8)	(9.0)	(17.1)
Age			16.2*			8.2			5.9			2.4			44.8**
			(8.8)			(32.7)			(7.0)			(5.9)			(21.5)
Age^2			-0.1*			-0.0			-0.0			-0.0			-0.3*
			(0.1)			(0.3)			(0.1)			(0.0)			(0.2)
Controls?	No	Yes	Yes	No	Yes	Yes	No	Yes	Yes	No	Yes	Yes	No	Yes	Yes
N	1,836	1,833	1,833	1,836	1,833	1,833	1,836	1,833	1,833	1,836	1,833	1,833	1,836	1,833	1,833
R^2	0.01	0.03	0.03	0.03	0.06	0.06	0.00	0.02	0.02	0.00	0.01	0.01	0.01	0.03	0.04

NOTE: Survey weights used. Standard errors in parentheses. * p≤ 0.10; ** p≤ 0.05; *** p≤ 0.01. All models include control for survey year and a constant. Other controls are educational attainment, spouse age and its square, spouse educational attainment, and an indicator for presence of children in the household.

Table 4.3 Regression Analysis for Single Females (minutes per day)

A. Home production and related activities

	Home production			Housework			Food prep.			Maintenance, repair			Lawn & garden			Purchases, shopping		
Postretirement	16.8	14.5	37.1	20.7	19.8	44.8	4.3	5.0	10.1	-2.0	-2.2	-0.9	3.5	3.6	1.9	-5.4	-5.9	-20.8
	(18.9)	(18.8)	(50.8)	(14.1)	(13.8)	(36.7)	(7.0)	(6.7)	(17.0)	(5.2)	(5.8)	(15.3)	(5.9)	(5.6)	(15.6)	(5.9)	(7.0)	(16.8)
Age			79.6			16.5			60.8***			28.2**			-17.7			12.4
			(60.0)			(41.9)			(16.7)			(13.1)			(20.8)			(17.8)
Age^2			-0.6			-0.2			-0.5***			-0.2**			0.1			-0.1
			(0.5)			(0.3)			(0.1)			(0.1)			(0.2)			(0.1)
Controls?	No	Yes	Yes	No	Yes	Yes	No	Yes	Yes	No	Yes	Yes	No	Yes	Yes	No	Yes	Yes
N	456	456	456	456	456	456	456	456	456	456	456	456	456	456	456	456	456	456
R^2	0.00	0.04	0.05	0.01	0.08	0.08	0.00	0.04	0.07	0.00	0.02	0.02	0.01	0.03	0.04	0.01	0.01	0.02

B. Other production

	Volunteer work			Care for/help others			Market work			Travel		
Postretirement	-1.8	-2.4	-15.3	-2.8	4.2	40.3	-141.2***	-135.4***	-82.1	-16.7**	-14.2*	9.7
	(3.8)	(4.2)	(14.2)	(10.1)	(9.2)	(37.9)	(24.9)	(24.7)	(60.8)	(7.8)	(8.6)	(19.4)
Age			22.4*			6.3			21.7			-1.0
			(12.1)			(37.2)			(66.0)			(24.0)
Age^2			-0.2*			-0.1			-0.2			-0.0
			(0.1)			(0.3)			(0.5)			(0.2)
Controls?	No	Yes	Yes	No	Yes	Yes	No	Yes	Yes	No	Yes	Yes
N	456	456	456	456	456	456	456	456	456	456	456	456
R^2	0.01	0.05	0.07	0.00	0.06	0.07	0.09	0.14	0.14	0.01	0.07	0.07

C. Consumption

	Eating & drinking			Socialize, relax, leisure			Sports, exercise, recreation			Religious			Personal care		
Post-retirement	12.4**	13.9***	18.4	97.2***	93.0***	−15.1	1.8	1.3	8.9	4.8	5.5*	0.7	43.6**	35.7**	28.1
	(5.1)	(5.2)	(13.4)	(24.3)	(23.8)	(62.9)	(2.8)	(2.5)	(9.6)	(3.2)	(3.2)	(8.1)	(18.9)	(17.1)	(42.4)
Age			2.1			−135.3*			9.5			−9.8			−37.8
			(14.6)			(71.5)			(8.9)			(10.4)			(46.5)
Age²			−0.0			1.2**			−0.1			0.1			0.3
			(0.1)			(0.6)			(0.1)			(0.1)			(0.4)
Controls?	No	Yes	Yes	No	Yes	Yes	No	Yes	Yes	No	Yes	Yes	No	Yes	Yes
N	456	456	456	456	456	456	456	456	456	456	456	456	456	456	456
R²	0.03	0.06	0.06	0.05	0.07	0.08	0.02	0.06	0.07	0.01	0.02	0.02	0.02	0.08	0.08

NOTE: Survey weights used. Standard errors in parentheses. * p≤ .10; ** p≤ .05; *** p≤ .01. All models include control for survey year and a constant. Other controls are educational attainment, spouse age and its square, spouse educational attainment, and an indicator for presence of children in the household.

Table 4.4 Regression Analysis for Partnered Males (minutes per day)

A. Home production and related activities

	Home production			Housework			Food prep.			Maintenance, repair			Lawn & garden			Purchases, shopping		
Postretirement	19.2**	23.0**	32.3	3.2	6.6*	11.6*	5.8**	10.0***	4.9	-4.9	2.2	13.8	13.9***	6.4	2.1	6.6***	7.9***	4.5
	(8.3)	(11.6)	(20.5)	(2.4)	(3.6)	(5.4)	(2.5)	(3.3)	(5.2)	(4.9)	(8.2)	(12.0)	(4.9)	(5.8)	(11.8)	(2.2)	(2.9)	(5.5)
Age			9.3			-5.3			-9.6			11.9			13.1			-0.2
			(24.0)			(6.1)			(6.6)			(14.1)			(13.2)			(6.4)
Age²			-0.1			0.0			0.1			-0.1			-0.1			0.0
			(0.2)			(0.0)			(0.1)			(0.1)			(0.1)			(0.1)
Controls?	No	Yes	Yes	No	Yes	Yes	No	Yes	Yes	No	Yes	Yes	No	Yes	Yes	No	Yes	Yes
N	1,911	1,908	1,908	1,911	1,908	1,908	1,911	1,908	1,908	1,911	1,908	1,908	1,911	1,908	1,908	1,911	1,908	1,908
R²	0.00	0.02	0.02	0.00	0.01	0.01	0.01	0.02	0.02	0.00	0.01	0.01	0.01	0.02	0.02	0.01	0.02	0.02

B. Other production

	Volunteer work			Care for/help others			Market work			Travel		
Postretirement	4.7**	2.1	2.0	7.0*	5.9	17.7	-193.7***	-155.4***	-120.2***	-3.6	0.4	-2.5
	(2.2)	(2.6)	(5.2)	(4.2)	(5.5)	(14.1)	(14.3)	(18.7)	(37.1)	(3.9)	(5.0)	(10.4)
Age			-5.8			28.2**			-6.1			4.0
			(7.1)			(12.8)			(44.5)			(12.0)
Age²			0.0			-0.2**			0.0			-0.0
			(0.1)			(0.1)			(0.3)			(0.1)
Controls?	No	Yes	Yes	No	Yes	Yes	No	Yes	Yes	No	Yes	Yes
N	1,911	1,908	1,908	1,911	1,908	1,908	1,911	1,908	1,908	1,911	1,908	1,908
R²	0.00	0.03	0.03	0.00	0.01	0.01	0.12	0.16	0.16	0.00	0.01	0.01

C. Consumption

	Eating & drinking			Socialize, relax, leisure			Sports, exercise, recreation			Religious			Personal care		
Post-retirement	11.1***	12.8***	7.8	108.6***	76.6***	49.1*	−1.9	−5.5	−9.6	4.0**	3.4	−3.8	26.1***	19.6**	12.8
	(2.8)	(4.0)	(7.7)	(11.6)	(15.6)	(29.3)	(3.3)	(4.5)	(8.8)	(1.9)	(2.3)	(4.3)	(6.9)	(9.9)	(19.1)
Age			.01			−8.7			7.3			−6.5			−30.3
			(8.9)			(35.8)			(10.6)			(5.4)			(22.2)
Age^2			0.0			0.1			−0.1			.01			0.2
			(0.1)			(0.3)			(0.1)			(0.0)			(0.2)
Controls?	No	Yes	Yes	No	Yes	Yes	No	Yes	Yes	No	Yes	Yes	No	Yes	Yes
N	1,911	1,908	1,908	1,911	1,908	1,908	1,911	1,908	1,908	1,911	1,908	1,908	1,911	1,908	1,908
R^2	0.01	0.03	0.03	0.06	0.13	0.13	0.00	0.01	0.01	0.00	0.01	0.01	0.01	0.03	0.03

NOTE: Survey weights used. Standard errors in parentheses. * $p \leq 0.10$; ** $p \leq 0.05$; *** $p \leq 0.01$. All models include control for survey year and a constant. Other controls are educational attainment, spouse age and its square, spouse educational attainment, and an indicator for presence of children in the household.

Table 4.5 Regression Analysis for Single Males (minutes per day)

A. Home production and related activities

	Home production			Housework			Food prep.			Maintenance, repair			Lawn & garden			Purchases, shopping		
Postretirement	-10.1	-20.4	42.3	-4.5	-6.8	7.8	3.9	0.4	18.9	14.3	15.3	-8.2	1.0	2.6	-1.1	-0.2	-1.4	-22.1
	(32.7)	(37.5)	(62.5)	(7.2)	(8.2)	(21.7)	(7.6)	(7.8)	(16.7)	(13.0)	(13.4)	(22.2)	(13.8)	(14.1)	(31.0)	(8.8)	(9.7)	(25.6)
Age		-43.1			34.2			38.1**			-35.2			3.9			28.6	
		(90.8)			(22.5)			(16.4)			(40.7)			(41.0)			(21.6)	
Age²		0.03			-0.3			-0.3**			0.3			-0.0			-0.2	
		(0.7)			(0.2)			(0.1)			(0.4)			(0.3)			(0.2)	
Controls?	No	Yes	Yes	No	Yes	Yes	No	Yes	Yes	No	Yes	Yes	No	Yes	Yes	No	Yes	Yes
N	152	152	152	152	152	152	152	152	152	152	152	152	152	152	152	152	152	152
R²	0.01	0.14	0.15	0.01	0.06	0.07	0.02	0.13	0.16	0.03	0.05	0.07	0.01	0.09	0.09	0.00	0.04	0.06

B. Other production

	Volunteer work			Care for/help others			Market work			Travel		
Postretirement	-4.9*	-4.1	5.3	-9.0	-7.8	-44.2*	-48.7	-16.9	-222.6*	-9.6	3.3	-77.8*
	(2.6)	(2.7)	(4.9)	(6.7)	(7.9)	(26.5)	(58.8)	(49.2)	(119.1)	(13.4)	(11.4)	(45.0)
Age		5.9			57.0**			-211.8			35.9	
		(6.9)			(23.7)			(161.3)			(43.9)	
Age²		-0.1			-0.4**			1.9			-0.2	
		(0.1)			(0.2)			(1.3)			(0.3)	
Controls?	No	Yes	Yes	No	Yes	Yes	No	Yes	Yes	No	Yes	Yes
N	152	152	152	152	152	152	152	152	152	152	152	152
R²	0.05	0.10	0.11	0.00	0.04	0.10	0.04	0.19	0.22	0.00	0.11	0.17

C. Consumption

	Eating & drinking			Socialize, relax, leisure			Sports, exercise, recreation			Religious			Personal care		
Postretirement	0.1	6.1	4.5	69.0	31.3	248.6**	0.9	2.4	3.4	15.8	14.1	5.0	-25.2	-34.4	32.2
	(10.4)	(9.9)	(21.4)	(51.4)	(51.1)	(117.4)	(8.1)	(7.8)	(22.8)	(10.7)	(9.8)	(14.0)	(31.5)	(33.4)	(82.6)
Age			34.6			-42.9			19.2			-24.1			36.2
			(23.3)			(150.6)			(20.6)			(23.5)			(99.6)
Age²			-0.3			0.2			-0.2			0.2			-0.3
			(0.2)			(1.2)			(0.2)			(0.2)			(0.8)
Controls?	No	Yes	Yes	No	Yes	Yes	No	Yes	Yes	No	Yes	Yes	No	Yes	Yes
N	152	152	152	152	152	152	152	152	152	152	152	152	152	152	152
R²	0.00	0.08	0.10	0.04	0.14	0.18	0.00	0.11	0.12	0.03	0.05	0.06	0.01	0.05	0.06

NOTE: Survey weights used. Standard errors in parentheses. * p≤ 0.10; ** p≤ 0.05; *** p≤ 0.01. All models include control for survey year and a constant. Other controls are educational attainment, spouse age and its square, spouse educational attainment, and an indicator for presence of children in the household.

single men spend less time in market work and travel and more time socializing, relaxing, and taking leisure at postretirement ages relative to younger ages.

Partnered versus Single Comparisons

Differences between partnered and single persons are not formally tested here, so comparisons noted are based solely on point estimates. As previously mentioned, there are few significant results in the single-person samples. This is likely due in large part to the small size of these samples. It does appear from these results, however, that partnered individuals increase home production time in postretirement ages, while single persons may not, at least in specifications that do not control for age trends. However, if linear and quadratic age controls are included, then it appears that single women increase home production and housework time and decrease market work time even more than partnered women. Single women also appear to increase time spent eating and drinking; socializing, relaxing, and taking leisure; in sport, exercise, and recreation; and in personal care more so than partnered women.

Comparing partnered men to single men, after controlling for age trends, single men appear to increase food preparation time and overall home production time more than partnered men after retirement, and to decrease market work time more than partnered men in postretirement ages.

These comparisons do not provide strong evidence that partnered individuals are making larger adjustments in home production time than singles. Thus, there is not strong evidence here that marital bargaining is playing a large role in the shifts in time allocation after versus before retirement.

DISCUSSION AND CONCLUSION

This chapter presents some descriptive evidence that home production time increases after retirement. This is consistent with economic theory on the allocation of time: as the opportunity cost of time falls at retirement, the implied price of home produced goods falls relative to market-produced substitutes. Therefore, we should expect that time allocated to home production will rise while money expenditures fall. Both partnered men and women increase home production time. The absolute increase is larger for women—33.7 minutes per day relative to men's 23 minutes per day—but the percentage increase for men is larger—22 percent relative to 20 percent.[3] This implies about a 21 percent increase in home production time at the household level when both partners move into retirement ages. This is a substantial change, and could plausibly explain the decreases in money expenditures after retirement that have been found in various studies.

These findings are consistent with an increase in the substitution of home production time for money expenditures on goods and services after retirement. Zick and Bryant (2008) find that home production time serves to decrease income inequality among households in 1975 and in 2003. By adding the value of household production to money income, Zick and Bryant find that home-production time increases the total consumption possibilities of households with lower incomes relatively more than households with higher money incomes. To the contrary, Hamermesh (2008) finds that households that spend more money on food also spend more time on food, suggesting that time and money are not easily substituted, at least with regard to food. However, Hamermesh does not include postretirement-age individuals in his sample, and the model used may not accommodate well the large discrete shift that we might expect to occur in home production at retirement.

I find here that consumption time also increases in postretirement ages. Time spent in social and leisure activities, and time spent eating and drinking also increases. This implies additional substitution in consumption, adding to the argument that the overall level of well-being, and thus marginal utility of consumption, may not change discretely at retirement, unlike the conclusion drawn in studies based on expenditure data.

We cannot necessarily interpret the "effects" reported here as causal. For example, an increase in home production time may not be "caused by" retirement, but rather jointly chosen with retirement timing. If we were to impose retirement on individuals unexpectedly, then responses may be very different from changes that are found here. The interpretation offered here is that individuals may voluntarily decrease money expenditures and make up for that decrease by increasing home production time and more time-intensive forms of consumption, such as leisure. Thus, there may not be a discrete drop in welfare at retirement, as expenditure-based studies suggest. However, it is also plausible that individuals may increase home production out of need rather than choice if they have undersaved and are surprised by this realization at retirement age. These data cannot distinguish between those two interpretations.

While these estimates are primarily descriptive, they present strong suggestive evidence that time spent in both production and consumption increases after retirement. Future research planned by this author will explore these changes in greater detail.

Appendix 4A
Economic Theory of the Life Cycle

In a simple life-cycle model of consumption, individuals maximize utility over n periods given W, the present discounted value of lifetime income, and the real market rate of interest, r:

$$\max U = U\left(c_1, c_2, ..., c_n\right) = u\left(c_1\right) + u\left(c_2\right) + ... + u\left(c_n\right);$$

$$s.t. W = c_1 + \frac{c_2}{1+r} + ... + \frac{c_n}{\left(1+r\right)^{n-1}}.$$

If the sub-utility function $u(c_i)$, is invariant to time, so that future consumption is not discounted an individual will optimize by smoothing his or her marginal utility of consumption over time:

$$MU_{c_i} = \left(1+r\right)^{j-i} MU_{c_j} \quad \forall i < j.$$

In the presence of a positive real interest rate, consumption would increase in a smooth gradual fashion over the lifetime. However, the period-specific utility function may change as one ages so that, holding consumption constant, one's marginal utility may either rise or fall with age.

Notes

1. There is a difference in this category when using the three-year age range on either side of retirement ages. In that sample, women significantly decrease time in religious activities and men's time in this activity does not change.
2. I classify those living with a spouse or partner as "partnered" and those not living with a spouse or partner as "single," regardless of marital status.
3. These percentages are calculated based on mean times for men or women from Table 4.1 and from the second specification in Tables 4.2 and 4.4.

References

Banks, James, Richard Blundell, and Sara Tanner. 1998. "Is There a Retirement Savings Puzzle?" *American Economic Review* 88(4): 769–788.

Becker, Gary S. 1973. "Theory of Marriage: Part I." *The Journal of Political Economy* 81(4): 813–846.

———. 1988. "A Theory of the Allocation of Time." In *Neoclassical Microeconomics* 1: Schools of Thought in Economics series, no. 3. Aldershot, U.K.: Elgar, pp. 45–69.

Bernheim, B. Douglas, Jonathan Skinner, and Steven Weinberg. 2001. "What Accounts for the Variation in Retirement Wealth Among Households?" *American Economic Review* 91(4): 832–857.

Frazis, Harley, and Jay Stewart. 2006. "How Does Household Production Affect Earnings Inequality? Evidence from the American Time Use Survey." U.S. Bureau of Labor Statistics Working Paper no. 393. Washington, DC: U.S. Bureau of Labor Statistics. http://www.bls.gov/ore/abstract/ec/ec060050.htm (accessed November 21, 2007).

Gustman, Alan L., and Thomas L. Steinmeier. 2005. "The Social Security Early Entitlement Age in a Structural Model of Retirement and Wealth." *Journal of Public Economics* 89(2–3): 441–463.

Haider, Steven, and Melvin Stephens. 2004. "Is There a Retirement-Consumption Puzzle? Evidence Using Subjective Retirement Expectations." NBER Working Paper no. 10257. Cambridge, MA: National Bureau of Economic Research.

Hamermesh, Daniel S. 1984. "Consumption During Retirement: The Missing Link in the Life Cycle." *Review of Economics and Statistics* 66(1): 1–7.

———. 2008. "Direct Estimates of Household Production." *Economics Letters* 98(1): 31–34.

Laibson, David. 1998. "Life-Cycle Consumption and Hyperbolic Discount Functions." *European Economic Review* 42(3-5): 861–871.

Lillard, Lee, and Yoram Weiss. 1997. "Uncertain Health and Survival: Effect on End-of Life Consumption." *Journal of Business and Economic Statistics* 15(2): 254–268.

Lundberg, Shelly, Richard Startz, and Steven Stillman. 2003. "The Retirement-Consumption Puzzle: A Marital Bargaining Approach." *Journal of Public Economics* 87(6): 1199–1218.

Mariger, Randall P. 1987. "A Life-Cycle Consumption Model with Liquidity Constraints: Theory and Empirical Results." *Econometrica* 55(3): 533–557.

Robb, A.L., and J.B. Burbridge. 1989. "Consumption, Income, and Retirement." *Canadian Journal of Economics* 22(3): 522–542.

Stillman, Steve, and Jennifer Ward-Batts. 2003. "Household Decision-Making and the Postretirement Consumption Decline: Evidence from the HRS." Unpublished manuscript. Claremont, CA: Claremont McKenna College.

Ward-Batts, Jennifer. 2007. "Bad Planning, Household Bargaining, or Household Production? A Closer Look at Retirement Consumption Decline." Unpublished manuscript. Claremont, CA: Claremont McKenna College.

Zick, Cathleen, and W. Keith Bryant. 2008. "Does Housework Continue to Narrow the Income Gap? The Impact of American Housework on Economic Inequality over Time." In *How Do We Spend Our Time? Evidence from the American Time-Use Survey*, Jean Kimmel, ed. Kalamazoo, MI: W.E. Upjohn Institute for Employment Research, pp. 57–79.

5
The Time Use of Nonworking Men

Jay Stewart

U.S. Bureau of Labor Statistics

Since the late 1960s, the fraction of prime-aged men who do not work for a period of one year or more has nearly quadrupled, increasing from 2.2 percent in 1967 to 8.2 percent in 2004.[1] Figure 5.1 illustrates this trend along with trends in the reasons for not working. Although most nonworking men are sick or disabled, a large and growing fraction are not. Most noticeable about this graph is the large increase in the Family Care and Retired categories. The Sick/Disabled category has increased as well, but the increase has been disproportionately larger in the other categories so that the percentage of nonworkers in this category has fallen from 77 percent to 58 percent.

Much of the past literature has focused on the reasons for the increase in the nonwork rate, with particular attention being paid to those who did not work because they were sick or disabled. The consensus is that supply factors, especially the liberalization of federal disability insurance regulations, contributed to the increase in the 1970s, while demand factors, mainly the relative decline in the demand for less-skilled workers, contributed to the increase in the 1980s.

Less attention has been paid to how these men spend their time and the related topic of how they support themselves. The time use of nonworking men is of interest because, from a resource utilization perspective, policy implications depend on the extent to which these men are substituting nonmarket work for market work. Nonworkers' access to income is of interest to policymakers who wish to assess the adequacy of income from government programs combined with other sources of income, including income from family members. For the present analysis, we are interested in access to income because it affects how nonworking men spend their time.

Figure 5.1   Trends in the Nonwork Rate of 25- to 54-Year-Old Men by Reason for Not Working

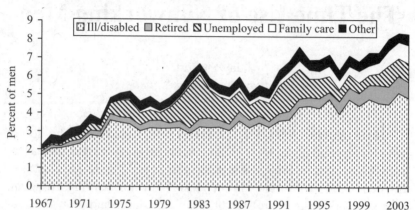

My analysis of nonworkers' time use will focus mainly on the division of time between leisure and household production activities, and how their time use differs from that of men who work.[2] Household production models, such as those in Becker (1965) and Gronau (1986), provide a theoretical framework for predicting how the time use of working and nonworking men differ and how other factors affect time use. Below, I briefly highlight the basic results from the Gronau model. A more rigorous discussion can be found in Appendix 5A.

The difference in workers' and nonworkers' time allocation is the sum of a substitution effect and an income effect. Because they do not forgo earnings when they spend time engaging in household production activities, nonworkers have a lower opportunity cost of time. This implies that they will consume fewer market goods and more home-produced goods (the substitution effect). Nonworkers also face a smaller budget set (have a smaller total income), which implies that they will spend less time in leisure activities (since leisure is a normal good) and more time doing household work.[3] Thus, both the income and substitution effects imply that nonworkers will spend more time doing household work than workers. In contrast, the difference in time spent on leisure activities is ambiguous. As with household work, a lower opportunity cost of time implies that nonworkers will spend more time in leisure activities. But, as noted above, nonworkers' lower incomes imply that they will spend less time in leisure activities. Thus, nonworkers could spend either more or less time in leisure activities depending on the relative magnitude of each effect.

There are other factors that could affect the comparison of workers' and nonworkers' time use. The discussion above assumes that workers and nonworkers have the same preferences and are equally productive at nonmarket work. However, it is possible that nonworkers have a stronger preference for leisure or nonmarket work or that they are more productive in nonmarket work. It can be shown that, under reasonable assumptions, individuals who are more productive in household production activities will spend more time in these activities. Thus, we would expect disabled nonworkers, who are likely less productive in household production, to spend less time doing household work. In contrast, the presence of children tends to increase the demand for household work. The productivity of time spent doing household work may also be higher because it is possible to look after children at the same time. Differences in the preference for leisure matter because those with a stronger preference will spend more time in leisure and less time in household production activities. Finally, greater amounts of unearned income or income from other family members will expand the budget set and tend to decrease the amount of time spent in household production activities and increase the time spent in leisure activities.

The outline for the rest of the chapter is as follows. I begin by updating what we already know about how nonworking men support themselves. Then I use data from the American Time Use Survey (ATUS) to examine how prime-age nonworking men spend their time and compare them to prime-age workers and older nonworkers.

SOURCES OF SUPPORT

Stewart (2006b) examines how prime-aged (25–54 years old) nonworking men supported themselves in the 1990s. In this section I update that analysis to cover the 2003–2004 period, which roughly coincides with the period covered by the ATUS data, using data from the 2004 and 2005 March Current Population Survey (CPS) files.[4] As in Stewart

(2006b), the focus of this section is on men who did not work at all during the calendar year.[5]

Sources of Income

Table 5.1 shows the percentage of nonworking men that had any unearned income and the percentage with each type of income by reason for not working. Most nonworkers (about 64 percent) had at least one source of unearned income, but there is considerable variation by reason for not working. Nonworkers in the Sick/Disabled or Retired categories, who comprise more than two-thirds of nonworkers, were by far the most likely to have unearned income. The percentages of nonworkers receiving income from each source are consistent with their reasons for not working. The most common sources of income for sick/disabled nonworkers were Social Security, disability benefits, and asset income, while asset and retirement income were the most common sources for retired nonworkers. The small fraction of retired nonworkers who received Social Security is due to the fact that they were too young for old-age benefits and were likely receiving Social Security Disability Insurance (SSDI) or Supplemental Security Income (SSI) payments. Unemployment benefits and asset income were the most common sources for those who were unable to find work, but relatively few received income from either of these sources. In the Family Care category, asset income was the most common source.

The amount of unearned income received (conditional on receiving any income) by reason for not working is shown in the top panel of Table 5.2, while the percentage of income from each source is shown in the bottom panel. The income amounts are before taxes and are deflated to 2004 dollars using the consumer price index. Conditional on having any unearned income, the average amount was $13,486, most of which came from Social Security and disability benefits.

Both average income and the percentage from each source vary considerably by reason for not working. Average income was highest for retired nonworkers, with about half coming from retirement sources (such as pensions) and another third coming from assets and Social Security. Sick/Disabled nonworkers' income was about the same as the overall average, although a much higher fraction—more than four-

Table 5.1 Percent of 25- to 54-Year-Old Male Nonworkers with Income from Various Sources, 2003–2004 Average

	All male nonworkers	Sick/disabled	Family care	Retired	Unable to find work	Other reasons
Percent of nonworking men	100.0	59.3	11.0	10.5	12.0	7.2
Percent of nonworking men with any unearned income	63.6	78.3	32.3	73.0	33.6	26.2
Percent of nonworking men with income from						
Assets	17.5	13.5	22.5	39.8	14.5	16.1
Disability sources	9.4	14.8	0.0	4.3	0.4	1.2
Social Security	39.6	60.4	3.3	29.0	2.4	1.9
Retirement plans	5.5	2.2	1.1	36.0	2.0	0.8
Unemployment compensation	4.5	2.8	4.3	0.6	16.8	4.6
Other sources	9.1	10.7	4.9	9.4	6.9	5.1
Observations	5,746	3,524	606	578	657	381

NOTE: The sample is from the March CPS and is restricted to civilian, noninstitutional men who did not work during the previous year. The top row shows the percent of nonworking men who report each reason for not working. The second row shows the percent of non-working men who have income from at least one source. The final rows show the percent of nonworking men who have income from each of the sources listed. These percentages do not add up to 100, because some nonworkers do not receive any income while others receive income from more than one source.

Table 5.2 Income of 25- to 54-Year-Old Male Nonworkers and Income of Other Adult Family Members Living in the Household, by Reason for Not Working, 2003–2004 Average

	All male nonworkers	Sick/disabled	Family care	Retired	Unable to find work	Other reasons
Percent of nonworking men with any unearned income	63.6	78.3	32.3	73.0	33.6	26.2
Mean unearned income (conditional on receipt) ($2004)	13,486	13,081	7,068	22,854	8,893	7,471
Percent of mean income (conditional on receipt) from						
Asset income	8.7	3.5	53.2	16.9	14.1	36.5
Disability income	17.9	23.6	0.0	4.4	4.1	8.0
Social Security income	46.4	58.4	9.8	21.4	4.6	10.7
Retirement income	12.7	2.5	11.8	48.4	15.1	5.4
Unemployment compensation	4.5	2.4	16.0	0.3	46.0	23.9
Other income	9.7	9.5	9.2	8.6	16.0	15.6
Total	100.0	100.0	100.0	100.0	100.0	100.0
Percent of nonworking men living with other adult family members that have income (earned or unearned)	61.6	59.1	70.3	66.3	66.5	53.4
Amount per other adult (conditional on receipt) ($2004)	21,647	18,756	35,506	23,870	19,853	19,757

NOTE: The sample is from the March CPS and is restricted to civilian, noninstitutional men who did not work during the previous year.

fifths—came from Social Security and disability benefits. Nonworking men who were unable to find work or were providing family care received considerably less income. Just under one-half of unemployed nonworkers' incomes came from unemployment benefits. For those providing family care, about half of their incomes came from assets, while unemployment compensation accounted for another 16 percent. The relatively large fraction of income coming from unemployment compensation could mean that some of these men are providing family care temporarily until they find work.

The bottom panel of Table 5.2 shows the percent of nonworking men living with other adult family members who received income (earned or unearned) during the year and the average amount per other adult (conditional on receipt). Here, family members include all immediate and extended family members living in the same household as the nonworker. Nonworkers who are providing family care are the most likely to be living with other adult family members with income, but there is surprisingly little variation across reasons. Average per-adult income is considerably larger for this group, which suggests that there is some specialization with the man staying at home.

Support from Family Members Living in the Household

It is clear from the preceding analysis that nonworkers' sources of income reflect the high proportion that are sick/disabled, that there is considerable variation in the incidence and amount of income received by reason for not working, and that a large fraction of nonworking men had little or no income. However, most nonworkers lived with other adult family members who received income, suggesting that family members are a possible source of financial support.

The top panel of Table 5.3 compares the distribution of workers and nonworkers across four types of living arrangement: no other family members present, living with a wife, living with parents, and living with other relatives. Compared with workers, nonworking men are less likely to be living with a spouse and are more likely to be living alone, with parents, or with other relatives. In the lower panel, which shows the distribution of living arrangements of workers and nonworkers by income, we can see that the differences are much smaller within income

116

Table 5.3 Distribution of Living Arrangements by Employment Status and Income, 2003–2004 Average

	No other family members in household	Living with wife	Living with parents[a]	Living with other relatives[a]	Total
All nonworkers	32.2	40.7	18.2	9.0	100
All workers	22.4	68.6	5.2	3.8	100
By income ($2004)					
Nonworkers					Percent
No income	26.3	35.7	25.6	12.4	100
1–10,000	38.7	36.0	17.9	7.5	100
10,001–25,000	33.2	49.8	10.3	6.7	100
25,001+	28.1	61.2	5.3	5.4	100
Workers					
1–10,000	31.0	45.2	15.6	8.2	100
10,001–25,000	30.1	54.1	9.2	6.6	100
25,001+	19.8	74.2	3.3	2.7	100

[a]No wife present.
SOURCE: Author's tabulations of March CPS data.

categories than overall. Moreover, differences in the distribution of living arrangements between income categories of nonworkers are larger than are the differences between workers and nonworkers within an income category. Thus, much of the difference between workers' and nonworkers' living arrangements is related to the differences in income rather than employment status per se. Because those with the lowest incomes are much more likely to be living with their parents or with "other relatives," these differences by income suggest that family members living with the nonworker could potentially be an important source of financial support.

The top panel of Table 5.4 shows the percentage of nonworking men that received income and the average amount conditional on receipt, by living arrangement. Nonworkers who lived alone or with their wives were about 40 percent more likely to have received unearned income compared with those living with their parents or with other relatives. Married nonworkers had the highest income conditional on receipt, while those living with their parents had the lowest.

The rest of Table 5.4 examines nonworking men's access to income. I assume that they had access to income if they or any family member living in the household received income during the year.[6] The percentage that has access from different relations varies predictably by living arrangement. The bottom panel shows the overall percentage of nonworkers that have access to income from other family members, and we can see that there is surprisingly little variation across living arrangements. Moreover, average total family income (conditional on receipt) is quite similar across living arrangements as well. Over all living arrangements, about 87 percent of nonworkers had access to income, either their own income or income from wives, parents, or other relatives. This also means that nearly 13 percent of nonworking men had no apparent means of support. There is no way to know how they financed their consumption, but there are several possibilities: they received income from nonfamily members that live in the household, they received unreported income from illegal activities or under-the-table jobs, they borrowed money, or they spent down their assets.

Table 5.5 accounts for differences in family size across living arrangements by showing family per capita income and the contributions to family per capita income from nonworkers, their spouses, parents,

Table 5.4 Percent of Male Nonworkers Who Have Access to Income (own income plus income of relatives living in household) and Amount Conditional on Access by Living Arrangement and Source of Income, 2003–2004 Average

	All male nonworkers	No other family members in household	Living with wife	Living with parents[a]	Living with other relatives[a]
Percent of nonworkers with unearned income	63.6	70.3	68.0	48.6	49.5
Average amount conditional on receipt ($2004)	13,486	13,103	15,227	9,696	12,092
Access to income (percent and average amount $2004)					
From wife	34.2		84.0		
	27,233		27,233		
From parents	18.8		3.8	95.0	
	27,502		20,462	28,127	
From other relatives	21.4		18.8	31.2	90.6
	24,115		18,663	21,785	30,884
Percent with access to income	87.4	70.3	94.6	97.6	95.3
Average total income conditional on receipt ($2004)	32,301	13,103	39,671	39,173	35,646
Percent of nonworking men	100.0	32.2	40.7	18.2	9.0
Observations	5,746	1,879	2,386	973	508

[a] No wife present.

NOTE: The sample is from the March CPS and is restricted to civilian, noninstitutional men who did not work during the previous year. The first entry in each living-arrangement-by-income-source cell is the percent of nonworking men in that living arrangement that received or had access to income from that source of income. The second entry is the amount conditional on receipt. For example, among nonworking men living with their wives, 84.0% had wives who received some income and the average amount of that income was $27,233. And 3.8% of nonworking men living with their wives had parents in the household who received income and the average amount of that income was $20,642. Any parents who did not receive income are not included in the 3.4%.

Table 5.5 Per Capita Income by Source and Type of Living Arrangement (conditional on receipt of income by the nonworker or any adult family member living with the nonworker), 2003–2004 Average

	All male nonworkers	No other family members in household	Living with wife	Living with parents[a]	Living with other relatives[a]
Mean per capita income ($2004)	12,471	12,452	12,753	12,500	11,182
Median per capita income ($2004)	8,906	8,340	9,010	9,841	8,635
Percent of mean per capita income from					
Male nonworker	44.2	100.0	30.1	14.2	21.3
Wife					
Earned income	23.6		52.4		
Unearned income	4.4		9.7		
Parents					
Earned income	7.9		0.6	37.6	
Unearned income	7.4		0.8	34.7	
Other relatives	12.6		6.5	13.5	78.7
Total	100.0	100.0	100.0	100.0	100.0

[a] No wife present.

NOTE: The sample is from the March CPS and is restricted to civilian, noninstitutional men who did not work during the previous year, and received unearned income or lived with related adults who received income (earned or unearned). Per capita income is computed by dividing the income of all adults living in the household who are related to the nonworker by the total number of related people who are living in the household.

and other relatives conditional on having any family income. Average per capita income was $12,471 over all living arrangements, and there was remarkably little variation across living arrangements, although per capita income was somewhat lower for nonworkers living with other relatives. Spouses provided about 60 percent of the income in married couples, with most of that being from earnings. When nonworkers lived with their parents (no wife present), the parents' income, about half of which was unearned, accounted for about 70 percent of per capita income.

The relatively small variation in the fraction of nonworking men who have access to income, and in the amounts conditional on having access, suggest that differences in time use across groups will be due more to differences in preferences or productivity in household production rather than differences in income.

HOW DO NONWORKING MEN SPEND THEIR TIME?

For this analysis, I pooled ATUS data from 2003, 2004, and 2005, and restricted the sample to men ages 25–54. Respondents were classified as workers or nonworkers based on the response to the ATUS labor force questions, although I dropped full-time students and the small fraction of nonworkers that reported working at a job on the diary day. Thus my sample consists of 11,560 men, of which 1,184 were not employed.

I collapsed the ATUS activity codes into five main activities: Work-Related Activities, Education, (unpaid) Household Work, Leisure and Sports, Personal Care, and Other Activities. Work-Related Activities include working at a job, activities done for a job, and job search activities; these activities exclude commuting and other work-related travel. Education includes taking classes (either for pleasure or for a degree), extracurricular activities, and homework. Household Work includes cleaning, meal preparation, shopping, yard work, household maintenance and repairs (plus travel related to household work), and child care (as a primary activity). Leisure and Sports includes watching TV, attending performances and sporting events, playing sports and games, doing hobbies, relaxing, and socializing. Personal Care includes sleeping and grooming. Other Activities include other travel, eating and drinking, phone calls, correspondence, and religious activities.

Table 5.6 shows the time spent in each of the five major categories (and selected detailed activities) by nonworkers and full- and part-time workers on an average day. For workers, the time spent in each activity is an average of both work and nonwork days. For nonworkers, of course, all days are nonwork days. Nonworking men spend about an hour more per day doing household work than men who are employed (either full or part time). They spend more time in meal preparation and doing housework, as predicted by theory, although these activities

Table 5.6 Time Use of Working and Nonworking Men, 2003–2005 Average (hrs./day)

	Nonworkers	Workers—average day	
		Part-time	Full-time
Work-related activities	0.23	4.21	6.29
Job search	0.23	0.05	0.01
Education	0.10	0.17	0.05
Household work	3.36	2.31	2.33
Housework	0.43	0.28	0.22
Shopping	0.34	0.27	0.30
Meal preparation	0.46	0.28	0.25
Lawn and garden	0.28	0.18	0.22
Child care	0.44	0.44	0.40
Leisure activities	7.87	5.35	4.16
Watching TV	4.62	3.00	2.18
Socializing	0.98	0.64	0.60
Relaxing	0.44	0.31	0.24
Sports participation	0.28	0.36	0.30
Personal care	10.05	9.53	8.68
Sleeping	9.36	8.96	8.04
Number of observations	1,184	474	9,902
Dissimilarity index comparison of nonworkers to workers		0.170	0.257

NOTE: The sample is from the ATUS and is restricted to civilian, noninstitutional men.

do not account for all of the difference between workers and nonworkers. Nonworkers spend about an hour and a half more in personal care, mostly sleeping, compared to full-time workers. However, the biggest difference in time use is in leisure time. Nonworking men spend nearly eight hours per day in leisure activities, with TV watching accounting for most of this. In contrast, full-time workers spend just over four hours per day in leisure activities, about half of which is TV watching. Part-time workers fall between full-time workers and nonworkers. Nonworkers also spend more time socializing, although it is important to note that time spent socializing while at work is not included for employed men.

Another way to think about the difference in time use between workers and nonworkers is to account for the time that is freed up by not working full time. The difference in time spent in work-related activities is about 6 hours per day. Of that freed-up time, about 17 percent (1 hour per day) is spent doing household work, 23 percent (1.4 hours per day) is spent in personal care activities, and 61 percent (3.7 hours per day) is spent in leisure activities. Thus, nonworkers do not seem to be substituting nonmarket work for market work to any great extent, so that the lion's share of the time that is freed up by not working is spent in leisure activities. These differences between workers and nonworkers are consistent with the predictions from economic theory, although we might have expected that household production would represent a larger fraction of freed-up time than leisure activities because the former was unambiguously predicted to increase.

These activity-by-activity comparisons make it clear that workers and nonworkers spend their time differently, but they do not tell us how differently. A convenient way to quantify differences in overall time use is to calculate a dissimilarity index.[7] This index ranges between 0 and 1 and is best described as the fraction of time that one group would have to reallocate to make the two groups identical. Thus, a value of 0 means that both groups spend the same amount of time in each activity, and a value of 1 means that the two groups have no activities in common. An index value of 0.05 or less indicates that there is virtually no difference between the two groups, 0.05–0.10 indicates a small difference, 0.10–0.15 indicates a moderate difference, and a value greater than 0.15 indicates a large difference.

The bottom row of Table 5.6 shows the index values for comparisons of nonworkers to part-time and full-time workers. The index values of 0.17 and 0.26 for comparisons to part-time and full-time workers indicate that there are large differences between the two groups, with the difference between nonworkers and full-time workers being considerably larger than the difference between nonworkers and part-time workers.

It is not too surprising that workers and nonworkers differ on an average day, because a large fraction of workers' days are spent in work-related activities. But how different are they when we restrict workers to their nonwork days? In Table 5.7, we can see that there is quite a bit

Table 5.7 Time Use of Working and Nonworking Men on Nonwork Days, 2003–2005 Average (hrs./day)

	Nonworkers	Workers, Nonwork days	
		Part-time	Full-time
Work-related activities	0.23	0.14	0.04
Job search	0.23	0.14	0.02
Education	0.10	0.27	0.10
Household work	3.36	3.26	4.54
Housework	0.43	0.48	0.51
Shopping	0.34	0.31	0.58
Meal preparation	0.46	0.33	0.40
Lawn and garden	0.28	0.24	0.48
Child care	0.44	0.51	0.63
Leisure activities	7.87	6.91	6.78
Watching TV	4.62	3.62	3.46
Socializing	0.98	0.93	1.00
Relaxing	0.44	0.60	0.36
Sports particpation	0.28	0.56	0.58
Personal care	10.05	10.75	10.03
Sleeping	9.36	10.33	9.45
Number of observations	1,184	195	3,653
Dissimilarity index comparison of nonworkers to workers		0.048	0.054

NOTE: The sample is from the ATUS and is restricted to civilian, noninstitutional men.

of similarity. Nonworkers spend about the same amount of time doing household work as part-time workers and about an hour per day less than full-time workers. Much of the difference between nonworkers and full-time workers on nonwork days is likely due to full-time workers' shifting of household work from workdays to nonwork days. The greater amount of childcare time spent by full-time employed men reflects the fact that men who work full time are more likely to be living with children in addition to the shifting of activities from workdays to nonworkdays. Nonworkers spend more time in leisure activities compared to men who work, but the difference is much smaller than on an average day. The dissimilarity index values at the bottom of Table 5.7 confirm these similarities. Both indexes are about 0.05, indicating that the days are very similar.

Now let's take a look at how time use varies by reason for not working. Table 5.8 shows that the differences in time use by reason are consistent with the economic model presented earlier. Disabled and retired nonworkers spend the least amount of time doing household work, while men who are providing family care spend the most. The relatively small amount of time spent doing household work by the disabled is consistent with lower productivity in household work for these groups. Given that nearly one-third of retired nonworkers receive SSI or SSDI, it is not too surprising that they spend their time much like the disabled. Nonworking men in the Family Care category differ from other nonworkers in that household production activities account for a much higher fraction of the time that is freed up by not working. They spend about the same amount of time doing household work as full-time employed men spend working for pay, although total work is greater for the latter group because they do household work as well. The greater amount of household work done by men in the Family Care category likely reflects specialization with the husband staying at home—men in this category are much more likely to be living in a household with children, as evidenced by the large amount of child care (more than four times as much as any other category).

The bottom portion of Table 5.8 compares overall time use by reason for not working. The dissimilarity index value of 0.06 for the comparison of disabled and retired nonworkers confirms the similarity of these two groups. Comparisons of the Family Care category to the other

Table 5.8 Time Use by Reason for Not Working, 2003–2005 Average (hrs./day)

	All non-workers	Reason for not working				
		Disabled	Unemployed	Family care	Retired	Other
Work-related activities	0.23	0.01	0.68	0.06	0.01	0.04
Job search	0.23	0.01	0.68	0.06	0.01	0.04
Education	0.10	0.07	0.07	0.10	0.00	0.30
Household work	3.36	2.41	4.08	6.54	2.95	3.87
Housework	0.43	0.41	0.39	1.26	0.27	0.45
Shopping	0.34	0.26	0.39	0.63	0.23	0.40
Meal preparation	0.46	0.37	0.52	1.08	0.46	0.44
Lawn and garden	0.28	0.17	0.33	0.02	0.51	0.45
Child care	0.44	0.28	0.52	2.12	0.08	0.46
Leisure activities	7.87	9.05	6.86	6.72	8.62	6.82
Watching TV	4.62	5.62	3.69	4.13	4.98	3.84
Socializing	0.98	0.93	1.08	0.77	0.67	1.04
Relaxing	0.44	0.60	0.35	0.19	0.33	0.29
Sports participation	0.28	0.21	0.34	0.17	0.39	0.35
Personal care	10.05	10.54	9.41	8.77	9.58	10.44
Sleeping	9.36	9.81	8.83	8.12	8.37	9.82
Number of observations	1,185	491	394	47	61	191
Dissimilarity index comparison of						
Disabled to…			0.138	0.175	0.061	0.097
Unemployed to…				0.104	0.080	0.052
Family care to…					0.156	0.112

NOTE: The sample is from the ATUS and is restricted to civilian, noninstitutional men.

categories confirm that this group is very different from disabled and retired nonworkers, but only slightly to moderately different from the unemployed.

Table 5.8 also shows that the unemployed spend about 0.7 of an hour per day in job search. This may not seem like very much, but it is consistent with stock-flow theories of job search.[8] Table 5.9 provides more detailed breaks for the unemployed. Men who are "looking for work" spend more time in job-search activities than men who are "on layoff," but not that much more. These two groups spend similar amounts of time doing household work, in leisure activities, and in personal care activities.

Table 5.9 Time Use of the Unemployed, 2003–2005 Average (hrs./day)

	On layoff	All	Long-term	Short-term	Unknown
			Looking for work		
Work-related activities	0.55	0.71	0.85	0.84	0.42
Job search	0.55	0.71	0.85	0.84	0.42
Education	0.02	0.08	0.11	0.00	0.16
Household work	4.24	4.03	3.30	4.65	3.90
Housework	0.32	0.41	0.41	0.40	0.43
Shopping	0.39	0.38	0.49	0.33	0.38
Meal preparation	0.59	0.50	0.41	0.46	0.63
Lawn and garden	0.47	0.29	0.10	0.50	0.22
Child care	0.36	0.58	0.66	0.62	0.43
Leisure activities	6.91	6.87	7.42	6.26	7.11
Watching TV	3.68	3.71	3.69	3.30	4.20
Socializing	0.78	1.16	1.41	1.13	1.03
Relaxing	0.31	0.36	0.19	0.33	0.53
Sports participation	0.60	0.27	0.32	0.20	0.33
Personal care	9.39	9.41	9.52	9.32	9.47
Sleeping	8.86	8.82	8.81	8.91	8.75
Number of observations	83	311	81	116	114
Dissimilarity index comparison of short-term unemployed to...	0.031		0.062		0.049

NOTE: The sample is from the ATUS and is restricted to civilian, noninstitutional men.

Greater differences appear when we distinguish between long-term and short-term unemployed (looking for work).[9] Short-term unemployed had a job at the time of their final CPS interview, which was 2–5 months prior to the ATUS interview. Long-term unemployed have not worked for at least a year, based on information from their final CPS interview. The Unknown category includes men who were not working at the time of the final CPS interview, but were not identified as being long-term nonworkers. Presumably they fall somewhere between long-term and short-term, but there is no way to know for sure. Long- and short-term unemployed spend similar amounts of time looking for work. But the long-term unemployed spend less time doing household work and more time in leisure activities. Perhaps not surprisingly, the dissimilarity index comparisons indicate that the short-term unemployed who are looking for work look more like those on layoff than they do like long-term job seekers, although all of the unemployed categories are fairly similar to each other.

Table 5.10 shows how time use varies by living arrangement. As noted above, the presence of children increases the demand for household work. Thus, it is not too surprising that nonworking men who live with their wives and children spend the most time doing household work and the least amount of time in leisure activities. Nonworking men who live with their parents or with other relatives spend the least amount of time doing household work and the most time in leisure activities. We know that nonworkers who live with their parents have the lowest incomes, which would lead one to believe that they would spend more time doing household work. But working in the opposite direction is the fact that they have access to income through their parents. It is possible that nonworking men who live with their parents are less productive in household work, but it seems more likely that they have a stronger preference for leisure activities.

Finally, Table 5.11 compares the time use of 25–54-year-old nonworkers to retirement-age (55+) nonworking men. Each entry shows the difference between younger (25–54) and older (55+) nonworkers in the amount of time spent in different activities by reason for not working. The differences between the two groups are rather small. Comparing time use activity-by-activity, we see that the largest difference is for time spent in leisure activities, with younger nonworking men spending

Table 5.10 Time Use by Type of Living Arrangement, 2003–2005 Average

	All nonworkers	No other family members in household	Living arrangement			
			Living with wife	Living with wife and children	Living with parents[a]	Living with other relatives[a]
Work-related activities	0.23	0.19	0.12	0.41	0.15	0.34
Job search	0.23	0.19	0.12	0.41	0.15	0.34
Education	0.10	0.12	0.08	0.08	0.15	0.00
Household work	3.36	2.47	3.81	4.87	2.28	2.25
Housework	0.43	0.41	0.44	0.55	0.29	0.33
Shopping	0.34	0.27	0.39	0.35	0.40	0.31
Meal preparation	0.46	0.40	0.44	0.62	0.37	0.15
Lawn and garden	0.28	0.19	0.44	0.32	0.22	0.01
Child care	0.44	0.13	0.00	1.40	0.06	0.12
Leisure activities	7.87	8.28	7.85	6.79	8.85	8.28
Watching TV	4.62	4.99	4.38	3.85	5.61	3.79
Socializing	0.98	1.06	0.85	1.11	0.75	0.65
Relaxing	0.44	0.41	0.37	0.38	0.56	1.46
Sports participation	0.28	0.33	0.31	0.22	0.27	0.27
Personal care	10.05	10.34	9.57	9.77	10.51	9.60
Sleeping	9.36	9.69	8.80	9.02	10.00	8.73
Number of observations	1,184	479	176	374	114	41

NOTE: The sample is from the ATUS and is restricted to civilian, noninstitutional men.
[a] No wife present.

Table 5.11 Comparison of Younger Nonworkers' (25–54) and Older Nonworkers' (55+) Time Use, 2003–2005 Aver-

	All nonworkers	Reason for not working				
		Disabled	Unemployed	Family care	Retired	Other
Work-related activities	0.21	0.00	0.10	—	0.01	0.02
Job search	0.21	0.00	0.10	—	0.01	0.02
Education	0.08	0.03	-0.01	—	-0.02	0.30
Household work	0.29	0.46	0.10	—	-0.22	0.59
Housework	0.14	0.09	-0.07	—	-0.02	0.31
Shopping	-0.05	-0.03	-0.02	—	-0.16	-0.08
Meal preparation	0.05	-0.02	-0.10	—	0.06	0.06
Lawn and garden	-0.27	-0.08	-0.30	—	-0.07	-0.47
Child care	0.42	0.26	0.49	—	0.06	0.44
Leisure activities	-0.56	-0.46	-0.38	—	0.30	-2.20
Watching TV	0.01	-0.49	-0.69	—	0.57	-1.28
Socializing	0.18	0.04	0.40	—	-0.12	0.07
Relaxing	-0.33	-0.41	-0.03	—	-0.41	-0.75
Sports participation	-0.10	-0.01	0.05	—	-0.01	-0.08
Personal care	0.43	0.29	0.52	—	-0.02	1.73
Sleeping	0.40	0.48	0.36	—	-0.58	1.54
Number of observations (55+)	3,409	354	115	4	2,857	79
Dissimilarity index comparison of nonworkers aged 25–54 and 55+	0.042	0.033	0.030		0.013	0.110

NOTE: The sample is from the ATUS and is restricted to civilian, noninstitutional men. A dash indicates that there were not enough observations to generate an estimate.

about one-half hour less time in leisure activities compared to older nonworkers. Overall time use, as measured by the dissimilarity index, is very similar for younger and older nonworkers. When time use is broken down by reason for not working, the two groups look more similar except for the Other Reasons category.

The small differences between older and younger nonworkers is consistent with the findings in a recent study by Krantz-Kent and Stewart (2007) that the time use of the elderly depends more on employment status than on age per se. It is also important to note that older individuals in the ATUS are healthier on average than the population as a whole (Krantz-Kent and Stewart 2007).

SUMMARY AND CONCLUSION

There has been a dramatic increase in the fraction of men who do not work for extended periods of time over the past 35 years. Earlier research has examined sources of support, but relatively little is known about how nonworking men spend their time. This chapter updates what we know about how nonworking men support themselves and uses data from the new ATUS to examine how they spend their time.

Most nonworking men have at least some unearned income; of which Social Security is the most common source, reflecting the fact that most male nonworkers are disabled. Nonworking men with little income are less likely to be living with a spouse and are more likely to be living with their parents or with other relatives. For these low-income nonworkers, family members living in the household are an important source of support. As a result, there is relatively little variation in access to income across living arrangements.

Economic theory predicts that, compared to workers, nonworking men will spend more time doing household work, but could spend either more or less time in leisure activities. The ATUS data revealed that most of the time that is freed up by not working full time is spent in leisure activities—very little of it is spent doing household work. The average day of a nonworking man looks much like the average day off of a full-time worker. Time use varies predictably by reason for not working. The disabled and retired spend the most time in leisure activities and the least amount of time doing household work. Men providing family care spend as much time doing household work as full-time employed men spend working for pay. The unemployed spend relatively little time looking for work, and fall between the disabled and those providing family care in the amount of time they spend doing household work. Finally, prime-age nonworking men spend their time much like retirement-age nonworkers, which is consistent with the findings of an earlier study that shows that employment status is a more important factor than age in explaining time use.

Appendix 5A
Predictions from Economic Theory

Gronau (1986) provides a useful model for examining differences in how workers and nonworkers use their time. The Gronau model differs from standard labor supply models in that goods may be purchased in the market or produced at home, and the time spent not working in the market can be spent in leisure activities or in household production activities.[1] I present the model for a single-person household, and later discuss how things change when there are other people in the household. Using Gronau's notation, the utility function is given as

$$U = U(X,L,H,N),$$

where X is the value of goods and services purchased in the market plus those produced at home, L is time spent in leisure, H is time spent in household production, and N is time spent working for pay. The individual maximizes utility subject to the following constraints:

$$X = X_M + f(H) = W \times N + V + f(H) \ ;$$

$$T = L + H + N,$$

where X_M represents the value goods and services purchased in the market, W is the individual's market wage, V is unearned income, and $f(H)$ is the home production function ($f_H > 0$ and $f_{HH} < 0$). The first constraint states that the value of goods and services consumed by the individual equals the sum of earned and unearned income plus the value of goods and services produced at home. The second constraint states that the time spent in market work, nonmarket work, and leisure must equal the total time available.

There are several features of this model that are worth noting. First, as is evident from the first constraint, home-produced goods are perfect substitutes for market goods. This may seem unrealistic, because households clearly do not produce most of the goods that they consume.

133

An alternative way to specify the model would be to allow goods and services to enter into the production function separately, and to assume that home production is a perfect substitute only for services. Under this specification, the qualitative results are the same, so I used the simpler specification. Second, the time spent in market and nonmarket work enters directly into the utility function. This allows individuals to obtain utility or disutility from these activities. I assume that, at the margin, the marginal utility of time spent in these activities is negative, and that the disutility of work is concave ($U_H, U_N, U_{HH}, U_{NN} < 0$). Third, market goods do not enter into the production function. This is consistent with the notion that home production is a substitute mainly for services, but abstracts somewhat from reality in that much of this production would involve the use of household capital (vacuum cleaners, stoves, dish-washers, etc.) or market goods (food, cleaning supplies, etc.).

Figure 5A.1 illustrates the equilibrium for a nonworker. Goods are measured along the vertical axis and leisure time is measured along the horizontal axis. The curve labeled GT is the home production pos-

Figure 5A.1 Home Production Equilibrium—Not Employed

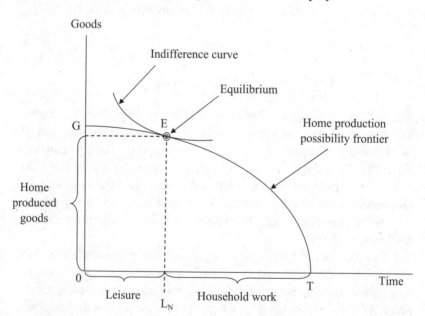

sibilities frontier (HPPF) for this individual, and shows attainable combinations of goods and leisure time. At point T, the individual spends all of his time in leisure and consumes no goods, while at point G the individual consumes 0G worth of goods (produced at home) and spends no time in leisure activities. The equilibrium for this individual is where his marginal rate of substitution between goods and leisure is equal to the marginal rate of transformation, which is the point at which his indifference curve is tangent to the HPPF (at point E).[2] The total amount of time available, 0T, is divided between leisure activities, $0L_N$, and household production, $L_N T$.

Figure 5A.2 shows the equilibrium for a worker. The individual's choice set is the same except for the addition of a wage line, which is tangent to the HPPF (at point H) and has slope equal to the negative of the wage rate. At the tangency point, the individual is equally productive in market and nonmarket work. At points to the right of point H the slope of the HPPF is greater than the slope of the wage line indicating

Figure 5A.2 Home Production Equilibrium—Employed

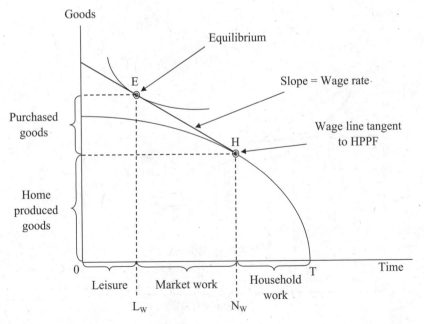

· that the individual is more productive doing nonmarket work, while to the left of H the individual is more productive in market work. Thus, the point of tangency between the HPPF and the wage line determines the amount of time spent in household production (shown by N_wT). The point of tangency between the indifference curve and the wage line determines the amount of time spent in leisure activities, $0L_w$. The time spent in market work is simply the remainder $(T - N_wT - 0L_w)$ or L_wN_w.

Finally, Figure 5A.3 compares workers and nonworkers. As drawn, nonworkers spend more time in both leisure and household production activities. However, if one works out the mathematics of the optimization problem it can be shown that it is only the time spent in household production that is unambiguously greater, because the income and substitution effects both work to increase the amount of time spent in household production activities. For leisure, the income and substitution effects work in opposite directions. The flatter slope of the budget

Figure 5A.3 Comparison of Employed and Not Employed

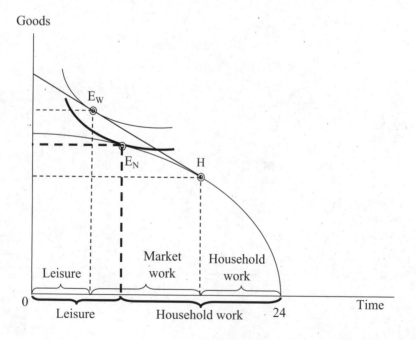

set to the left of point H means that time spent in nonleisure activities is less valuable and tends to increase the amount of time spent in leisure activities. But the smaller budget set leads the individual to spend less time in leisure activities.

There are a number of assumptions embedded in Figures 5A.1–5A.3. First, it is assumed that workers and nonworkers have the same preferences and are equally productive at nonmarket work, so that the only difference between them is that nonworkers' wages are so low that they choose not to work. However, it is also possible that nonworkers do not work because they have a stronger preference for leisure or non-market work or that they are more productive in nonmarket work. It can be shown that, under reasonable assumptions, individuals who are more productive in household production activities will spend more time in these activities. Thus we would expect disabled nonworkers, who are likely less productive in household production, to spend less time doing household work. In contrast, the presence of children tends to increase the productivity of time spent in household work, because they can look after their children at the same time. Thus we would expect nonworkers who live with children to spend more time doing household work. Differences in preferences for leisure matter, because those with stronger preferences for leisure will spend less time in household production activities. Finally, greater amounts of unearned income or income from other family members will shift up the HPPF (a pure income effect) and tend to reduce the amount of time spent in household production activities and increase the time spent in leisure activities.

Appendix Notes

1. In an earlier paper, Becker (1965) presents a model in which goods and leisure do not directly enter the utility function. Instead, households conbine time and market goods to produce commodities, from which household members derive utitily. For example, going to the movies is produced by combining purchased movie tickets (the market good component) and time spent going to the movie (which includes travel time to and from the theater and time spent waiting in line, in addition to the time actually watching the movie). The drawback to this approach is that it is impossible to derive testable implications about time spent in leisure and household production activities.
2. Recall that an indifference curve shows combinations of goods, in this case goods and leisure, that generate the same amount of utility.

Notes

1. Author's tabulation of March Current Population Survey (CPS) data.
2. Household production activities include doing housework, preparing meals, doing yard work, performing house or vehicle maintenance or repairs—anything that satisfies the "third-person criterion" that the same results could have been obtained if done by a third person (Reid 1934). To illustrate the third-person criterion, cooking a meal satisfies this criterion, but eating it does not. Throughout this essay, I will use the terms nonmarket work, household production, and household work interchangeably.
3. A normal good is one whose consumption increases as income increases.
4. The analysis of ATUS data in the next section covers the years 2003–2005. The 2006 March CPS data (covering 2005) were not available at the time I performed this analysis. However, adding the 2005 data likely would have little effect on the results.
5. See Stewart (2006b) for details on data and methods.
6. It is impossible to know how income is distributed among family members, and the implicit assumption is that income is distributed approximately equally.
7. I use the weighted absolute deviation index given below:

$$D = \sum_{i=1}^{6} \left\{ \frac{|a_i - b_i|}{a_i + b_i} \left(\frac{a_i + b_i}{\sum_{i=1}^{6}(a_i + b_i)} \right) \right\} \doteq \sum_{i=1}^{6} \left\{ \frac{|a_i - b_i|}{\sum_{i=1}^{6}(a_i + b_i)} \right\}$$

where a_i is the time spent in activity i by group a and b_i is the time spent in activity i by group b. For each comparison, I computed the index using the six major aggregated activities. See Stewart (2006a) for a more complete description of dissimilarity indexes.

8. According to these theories, immediately after individuals become unemployed, they spend a lot of time looking for work as they investigate the jobs that are available at that time. After this initial search activity, they only need to check for new job openings.
9. Those who are on layoff are, by definition, short-term unemployed.

References

Becker, Gary S. 1965. "A Theory of the Allocation of Time." *Economic Journal* 75(299): 493–517.

Gronau, Reuben. 1986. "Home Production—A Survey." In *Handbook of Labor Economics,* Orley Ashenfelter and Richard Layard, eds. Amsterdam: North Holland, pp. 273–304.

Krantz-Kent, Rachel, and Jay Stewart. 2007. "How Do Older Americans Spend Their Time?" *Monthly Labor Review* 130(5): 8–26.

Reid, Margaret G. 1934. *Economics of Household Production.* New York: Wiley and Sons.

Stewart, Jay. 2006a. "Assessing Alternative Dissimilarity Indexes for Comparing Activity Profiles." *The Electronic Journal of Time Use Research* 3(1): 49–59. http://ffb.unilueneburg.de/eijtur/pdf/volumes/eIJTUR-3-1 .pdf#pagemode=bookmark (accessed December 5, 2007).

———. 2006b. "Nonworking Men: Who Are They and Who Supports Them?" *Demography* 43(4): 537–552.

6

Day, Evening, and Night Workers

A Comparison of What They Do in Their Nonwork Hours and with Whom They Interact

Anne Polivka
U.S. Bureau of Labor Statistics

During the last several decades, dramatic shifts have occurred in the timing of economic activity. Grocery stores have extended their hours, mail orders for merchandise can be placed any time of day, and financial markets' hours have expanded with the increased electronic linkage of markets. Further, with the rising globalization of markets and the increasing demand for around-the-clock medical care necessitated by the aging of the U.S. population, it is likely that the expansion of the time frame in which economic activity takes place will continue. Some of the increase in economic activity conducted in these expanded hours has been accomplished through automated processes; however, much of this expanded activity continues to be done by people. Estimates from a supplement to the Current Population Survey indicate that in May 2004, almost 15 percent of full-time wage and salary workers usually worked a nondaytime shift (U.S. Department of Labor 2005).

This chapter uses data from the American Time Use Survey (ATUS) to examine how working atypical hours—evening and night shifts—affects the activities in which individuals engage and the amount of time they spend interacting with others. Part of the concern about evening and night shifts is that they may cause individuals who work these times to be less integrated with their communities and thus to have a noncongruent role in society. This lack of integration and incongruity arises, Dunham (1977) and more recently Hamermesh (1999) argue, because there are segments of the day that have fixed social value that cannot be easily changed. Most communities are oriented to some degree to a day schedule, thus businesses, recreational facilities, and governmental institutions are more likely to be open during daytime hours. In addition, social events, organizational meetings, volunteer activities, and school events are more likely to be scheduled during periods of time when the majority of workers—day workers—are available. Brown (1975) discusses having "culturally sanctioned" time available for social activities as being critical to one's integration into society. Individuals employed on evening shifts may have this time blocked off by working, while individuals working night shifts may have this culturally sanctioned time blocked off by sleeping. Consequently, working an evening or night shift could cause these workers to be out of sync with society. Similarly, evening and night workers may have fewer hours to spend with their spouses and a smaller number of nonwork hours when their children are at home and awake. In short, working an evening or night shift could interrupt the rhythms of life, and this disruption could raise the economic costs of working an atypical schedule. The assumption that these costs exist has long been the basis for the argument that nonday workers should receive a premium for working hours outside the standard social norm (Alexander and Apraos 1956; Kostiuk 1990).

On the other hand, if the time spent in various activities and interacting with others does not vary significantly by when individuals work, then the unattractiveness and costs of being a nonday worker—the disamenity of being an evening or night worker—could be small. Further, if the increased provision of services in nonstandard hours and advances in technology, such as the Internet or digital video recorders, have decreased the fixed temporal aspects of various activities, then the premium that might be paid for working a nonday schedule to offset the disamenities of this work schedule may have fallen over time. A decline in this premium, in turn, could have contributed to the rise in earnings inequality that has been observed in the United States since the early 1990s.

Given these opposing views of the potential costs of working atypical hours, it is important to compare across people on different shifts the amount of time spent in various activities and in interactions with others. These comparisons could shed light on the economic consequences of being a nonday worker and have important implications for social policies that could be adopted to accommodate evening and night workers.

The comparison also could provide some insights into whether the cost of working a nonday schedule has decreased over time, if it is established that activities that were thought to be rare or nonexistent during certain times of the day 25 years ago are now found to be prevalent.

BACKGROUND AND PREVIOUS RESEARCH

Although the term "24/7" has only recently entered our vernacular, nonday shift work has been an established employment practice for decades. Initially, nonday work schedules were adopted to meet the demands of the continuous manufacturing production process that arose in the early 1900s. Shift work's prevalence and acceptance was enhanced during the 1940s when around-the-clock schedules were needed to meet war-time production requirements (Dunham 1977). More recently, the increase in women's participation in the paid labor market and the concomitant transition of the U.S. economy toward a "24/7" service economy has maintained the demand for shift workers (Beers 2000; Presser 1995).

In the 1960s and 1970s, workers' responses to working nonday schedules were the subject of considerable research. Much of this research was case study analysis that focused on the physical and psychological health effects of working nonday schedules. For example, extensive research was conducted on the effects of working a night or rotating schedule on sleeping and eating disorders (Bryden and Holdstock 1973; Dunham 1977; Kleitman 1963; Tasto et al. 1978; Zedeck, Jackson, and Summers 1983). In general, these biologically based studies found that working a non-standard shift increased sleep disruptions, decreased the quality of sleep, raised the probability of experiencing gastrointestinal disorders, and caused chronic malaise. To a lesser extent, some of the 1960s studies also examined the effect of shift work on individuals' social interactions, and a few studies found that there were disruptions (e.g., Mott et al. 1965).

In the 1980s, studies of shift workers concentrated on the effect of working a nonday schedule on family dynamics and the division of labor within families. Staines and Pleck's (1984, 1986) studies of single mothers and married couples in 1977 found that nonday shift work was associated with problems scheduling family activities, higher levels of work/family conflicts, difficult family adjustments, and degradation in the quality of family life. White and Keith's (1990) national survey of married couples interviewed in 1980 and again in 1983 also found a modest negative effect of working a nonday schedule on the quality of a marriage. Further, White and Keith observed that having one spouse working a nonday schedule significantly increased the likelihood of divorce over this three-year period, even though the current effect on the quality of marriage was modest.

Using the 1979 Panel Survey of Dynamics, Morgan (1981) found that among working parents with children under the age of 12, over one-fourth reported that their means of obtaining child care was to work a different shift than their spouses. Presser (1986), using the Current Population Survey's 1982 Fertility Supplement to examine women aged 18–44, found that although marriage decreased the probability of women working a nonday schedule, the care of children by relatives— particularly fathers—was substantially larger when mothers worked a nonday shift rather than a day schedule. With regard to the division of labor within families, Presser's (1988, 1994) analyses of dual-earner married couples (using data that she collected in 1986 and 1987) indicated that having one spouse work a nonday schedule increased the total amount of housework done by both husbands and wives.

In the late 1990s and early 2000s, there were relatively few studies of the effects of working a nonday schedule, and what analysis was conducted concentrated on the demographic characteristics of shift workers, the expansion of day schedules to earlier and later in the day, the comparison of the incidence of shift work across countries, and indirect assumptions about how shift workers were spending their time (Hamermesh 1996, 1998, 1999; Presser 1995; Presser and Gornick 2005). Recently there has been an upsurge in the analysis of the effect of working nonstandard hours on care provided to children both in the United States and Canada (Bianchi, Wight, and Raley 2005; Connelly and Kimmel 2008; Rapoport and LeBourdais forthcoming). However, this work has focused on various aspects of child care, and the Connelly and Kimmel piece concentrated on the effect of working hours on the margin of the normal workday rather than shift schedules per se.

The ATUS provides a unique opportunity to examine, across a wide variety of people and a broad range of activities, how individuals on different types of shifts spend their time on the days they work. Using ATUS data, it is possible to document the incidence and characteristics of those working a nonday schedule, and to explore whether individuals on various work schedules engage in different types of activities. In addition, examination of ATUS data will provide up-to-date answers to questions about whether workers on nonday schedules spend more or less time with family and friends, and if the "quality" of time spent together is equal across shifts.

DATA DESCRIPTION AND DEFINITIONS

Data Source

As is discussed in more detail in other chapters of this book, the ATUS is a nationally representative monthly survey that collects information on how individuals in the United States age 15 and older spend their time. The information on how individuals use their time is collected in phone interviews during which respondents sequentially described each of their primary (or main) activities, along with the activities' durations. Each of these activities is subsequently coded into one of over 400 detailed activity categories. A comparison of the time spent in these activities across workers on different shifts, using ATUS data collected in 2003 and 2004, will provide information about the economic costs of working an atypical schedule.[1]

A salient feature of the ATUS for this analysis is that in addition to collecting information about what an individual was doing, the survey collects information on who was in the room or accompanying the individual during each activity, unless the activity was sleeping, grooming, or working a job at an individual's workplace. Using this "who" information in combination with individuals' recorded activities, it is possible to construct a measure both of the amount of time spent with friends and family members, and a measure of the proportion of time that individuals spent with their friends and family members engaging in specific activities. By comparing these measures, it is possible to gain additional insights into the cost of being a nonday worker.

Definition and Classification of Individuals' Work Shifts

The ATUS does not specifically ask individuals if they worked a day, evening, or night shift. However, using the ATUS information about when throughout the day individuals worked and the duration of their work spells, individuals can be classified as day, evening, or night shift workers. To be consistent with previous research (Hedges and Sekscenski 1979; Presser 1994; Wight, Raley, and Bianchi 2007), for the analysis in this chapter individuals are classified based on when they worked the majority of their hours. Specifically, those who worked half or more of their total hours between 8 a.m. and 4 p.m. were classified as day workers, those who worked half or more of their hours between 4 p.m. and midnight were classified as evening workers, and those who worked half or more of their hours between midnight and 8 a.m. were classified as night workers.[2] Using the majority of hours worked as the metric to classify individuals into shifts avoids difficulty in determining what are normal daytime starting times and avoids asymmetries that could arise between full-time and part-time workers.

To avoid classifying individuals based on supplemental activities that they did related to their work, only the hours that individuals worked at their place of employment were included in the determination of an individual's shift. Individuals' work activities that were not conducted at their place of employment (such as high school teachers grading papers at home) were excluded because individuals probably have more control over when these "extra" hours were worked, and the inclusion of these hours might bias workers' shift classification. The analysis in this chapter also was restricted to those who were age 16 and older, had only a single job, and were wage and salary workers (self-employed workers were excluded). Based on these criteria, 8,322 observations were used in the estimates presented below. Of these 8,322 observations, 6,891 were people classified as day workers, 920 were evening workers, and 511 were night workers.

ESTIMATES OF THE PROPORTION AND CHARACTERISTICS OF WORKERS IN VARIOUS SHIFTS

Table 6.1 contains weighted estimates of the proportion of workers classified as day, evening, or night workers generated using the ATUS data, along with selected demographic and job characteristics of workers in these shifts.[3] According to these estimates, almost one in five wage and salary workers worked a nonday schedule, with 11 percent working an evening shift and 6 percent working a night shift.[4]

The ATUS estimates also indicated that these nonday workers tend to be younger and poorer, and are more likely to be black and less-educated than day workers.[5] For example, a little more than 20 percent of evening workers and 17 percent of night workers were from families whose incomes were less than $20,000 a year, compared to only 10 percent of day workers. Almost 27 percent of evening workers were in the leisure and hospitality industry and 17 percent were in retail trade—two industries that tend to disproportionately employ low-skill, low-wage workers. In contrast, only 5 percent and 11 percent of day workers were employed in these two industries, respectively.

The ATUS estimates do indicate that those working an evening shift were much more likely to be enrolled in school than those working a day or night shift (26 percent of evening workers compared to only 8 percent of day workers and 10 percent of night workers), suggesting that evening work may provide a means for individuals to combine schooling and work, which in turn could make higher education accessible for some who might not otherwise be able to afford it. This suggests that for some shift workers their current economic status may only be temporary. In general, however, the descriptive statistics indicate that those working a nonday schedule tend to come from more economically disadvantaged situations than do those who work a day schedule.

If the analysis presented in the rest of the chapter supports the hypothesis that nonday workers spend less time in activities that could be beneficial to their health and welfare and/or spend less time interacting with others, this could indicate that these workers are incurring significant cost by working a nonday schedule. In turn, the statistics presented in this section describing who works as evening and night workers indi-

Table 6.1 The Proportion and Characteristics of Wage and Salary Workers in Day, Evening, or Night Shifts (%)

Variables	Day workers	Evening workers	Night workers
Proportion of workers	83.6	10.9	5.5
Sex			
Male	53.3	57.7	64.9
Female	46.7	42.3	35.1
Race			
White	84.4	80.7	77.2
Black	10.1	14.7	17.8
Asian	3.5	3.5	2.1
Other	2.0	1.1	2.9
Ethnicity			
Non-Hispanic	87.0	83.3	88.4
Hispanic	13.0	16.7	11.6
Age			
16–19	2.8	17.9	4.5
20–24	8.8	16.3	9.3
25–29	11.0	12.8	10.9
30–54	62.3	42.1	60.9
55–59	8.4	4.5	8.1
60–64	4.0	2.8	3.2
65 + years	2.8	3.5	3.1
Education			
Less than high school	10.7	24.5	14.6
High school diploma	31.0	32.2	38.8
Some college	26.6	29.0	34.1
College degree	20.6	11.1	10.5
Advance degree	11.1	3.2	2.0
Enrolled in school			
Yes	8.4	26.2	9.5
No	91.6	73.8	90.5
Marital status			
Single	40.4	63.2	49.2
Married	59.6	36.8	50.8

(continued)

Table 6.1 (continued)

Variables	Day workers	Evening workers	Night workers
Child in the household[a] (including siblings)			
No child	55.5	53.0	58.3
Child present	44.5	47.0	41.7
Parent (child in household)[b]			
Not a parent	61.7	72.9	67.4
Parent	38.4	27.1	32.7
Parent (household and non)[c]			
Not a parent	60.9	71.5	66.1
Parent	39.1	28.5	33.9
Number of children in household[a]			
None	55.5	53.0	58.3
One	19.3	22.2	17.2
Two	16.5	16.1	15.5
Three	6.4	6.3	6.1
Four	1.8	1.7	2.6
Five or more			
Family income ($)			
5,000–9,999	3.1	7.2	4.2
10,000–19,999	7.2	13.0	12.6
20,000–29,999	10.3	13.7	19.3
30,000–49,999	23.4	23.8	24.3
50,000–74,999	24.5	19.2	25.2
75,000 and over	31.5	23.1	14.4
Industry			
Agriculture, forestry, fishing, & hunting	1.1	0.4	0.7
Mining	0.5	0.0	0.4
Construction	7.5	1.1	2.5
Manufacturing	14.7	12.6	24.7
Retail trade	11.3	16.9	12.7
Wholesale trade	3.5	2.3	2.6
Transportation and utilities	5.1	4.9	12.2

(continued)

Table 6.1 (continued)

Variables	Day workers	Evening workers	Night workers
Industry			
Information	2.8	2.4	3.2
Financial activities	8.3	3.8	2.5
Professional and business services	8.6	6.0	6.5
Educational and health services	21.0	15.6	18.8
Leisure and hospitality	5.4	26.6	6.7
Other services	5.2	3.9	0.7
Public administration	5.0	3.6	5.8
Occupation			
Management business & financial	16.3	3.9	4.2
Professional and related	22.5	11.3	12.1
Service	12.0	36.9	21.6
Sales and related	9.0	14.8	8.9
Office and administrative support	15.4	9.5	13.4
Farming, fishing, and forestry	0.9	0.1	0.4
Construction and extraction	6.2	1.2	5.5
Installation, maintenance, and repair	4.7	1.2	5.5
Production	7.5	10.5	19.9
Transportation	5.6	10.6	12.5

[a] Since people age 16 and older can be surveyed, the estimate of workers who have children in the household under the age of 18 can include younger siblings.

[b] The estimate of workers who are parents (child in the household) is restricted to those who are a parent or a stepparent of child under 18 years old who is residing in the household.

[c] The estimate of workers who are parents (household and nonhousehold children) includes those who are a parent or a stepparent of a child residing in the household under the age of 18 and those who are parents or a stepparent of a child under the age of 18 who is not currently residing in the household (e.g., a noncustodial parent).

cate that if such costs do exist, they are likely borne by some of the most vulnerable or disadvantaged segments of U.S. society.

COMPARISON OF THE ACTIVITIES OF DAY, EVENING, AND NIGHT WORKERS

To explore whether working a nonday schedule alters workers' activities, the average amount of time within the 24-hour period between 4 a.m. and 4 p.m. spent by day, evening, and night-shift workers in various activities are estimated. If an individual did not spend any time within the 24-hour period in a specified activity, the person is included in the averages with a recording of zero hours in the activity. Table 6.2 contains the estimates of the average amount of time workers on various schedules spent in 21 major activities. In addition, to examine specific activities that may be disrupted by working a nonday schedule and to provide more information about changes nonday workers may have made to accommodate these schedules, the average number of hours that day, evening, and night workers spent in four more detailed activities are listed in Table 6.2. These detailed categories are the average number of hours spent Sleeping; Watching Television; Participating in Sports and Exercising; and Traveling to, from, or for Work. The Sleeping category is further divided into time actually spent sleeping (Asleep) and time spent trying to sleep (Sleeplessness).

To facilitate the comparison of the amount of time that day, evening, and night workers spent in various activities, the discussion of the 21 major activities and four more detailed activities is divided into five broad areas: 1) activities related to individuals' health, 2) activities related to the maintenance of a residence and care of family members, 3) activities related to the purchase of goods and services, 4) activities done in individuals' leisure, "free" time, and 5) other activities that may be specifically related to individuals' job schedules and the characteristics of day, evening, or night workers.

Table 6.2 Average Hours per Day Spent in Specified Activity, by Worker's Shift Categorization (2003 and 2004 data combined, based on a 24-hour day, wage and salary workers with only one job)

Variables	All	Day shift	Evening shift	Night shift
Personal care	8.45	8.38	8.78	8.80
Sleeping	7.63	7.57	7.90	8.08
Asleep	7.61	7.55	7.89	8.05
Sleepless	0.02	0.02	0.02	0.03
Household activities	0.96	0.93	1.03	1.18
Caring for and helping household members	0.35	0.35	0.28	0.34
Caring for and helping non-household members	0.08	0.08	0.07	0.14
Education	0.18	0.10	0.82	0.15
Consumer purchases	0.21	0.20	0.23	0.30
Professional and personal care services purchases	0.05	0.04	0.07	0.07
Household services purchases	0.01	0.01	0.01	0.01
Government services use and civic obligations	0.00	0.00	0.01	0.01
Eating and drinking	1.03	1.07	0.81	0.88
Socializing, relaxing, and leisure	2.83	2.79	2.80	3.37
Watching television	1.69	1.68	1.56	2.07
Sports, exercise, and recreation	0.19	0.19	0.19	0.17
Participating in sports, or exercise	0.16	0.16	0.18	0.16
Religious and spiritual activities	0.04	0.04	0.05	0.11
Volunteer activities	0.07	0.07	0.03	0.05
Telephone calls	0.08	0.07	0.11	0.11
Traveling	1.34	1.35	1.31	1.24
Traveling to, from or for work	0.68	0.70	0.58	0.54

(continued)

Table 6.2 (continued)

Variables	All	Day shift	Evening shift	Night shift
Working at job (at place of work)	7.85	8.03	7.11	6.70
Other income-generating activities	0.01	0.01	0.02	0.07
Job search	0.00	0.00	0.01	0.00
Work activities direct part of job	0.00	0.00	0.00	0.00
Work-related activities (except exercising as part of job)	0.01	0.01	0.02	0.01
Uncodeable	0.07	0.07	0.10	0.06

Time Spent in Activities Related to Individuals' Physical Health

The early concern surrounding evening and night work was that it would disrupt individuals' schedules in a manner that would adversely affect their health. There was particular concern that nonday schedules would affect both the quantity and quality of individuals' sleep. Contrary to these expectations, the ATUS estimates presented in Table 6.2 indicate that, at least with regard to the amount of time spent sleeping, these concerns are unfounded. On average, the ATUS estimates show that night workers slept a half hour more on the days that they worked than did day workers, while evening workers slept about 18 minutes longer than day workers. Further, to the extent that it is completely reported, the ATUS data indicate that night and evening workers were no more likely to spend large amounts of time trying to sleep when they could not than were day workers.

The estimates presented in Table 6.2 also indicate that working a nonday schedule does not influence the amount of time individuals spent exercising or participating in sports—another set of activities that generally is considered healthy. Regardless of their shift, workers on average spent very little time exercising on the days that they worked—less than 12 minutes a day. Estimates of the proportion of day, evening, and night workers who actually engaged in these activities also indicate few differences by shift. Only 15 percent of day workers, 12 percent of evening workers, and 12 percent of night workers participated in sports or exercised on their workdays.

In contrast, the estimates in Table 6.2 indicate that working a nonday schedule does affect the amount of time individuals spent eating. On the days that they work, evening workers spent approximately 18 fewer minutes and night workers spent approximately 12 fewer minutes eating than did day workers. Further investigation is necessary to determine whether the smaller amount of time spent eating by evening and night workers is due to fewer meals being eaten or less time being spent eating the same number of meals. To provide some insights into whether less healthy types of food are being eaten, there also needs to be a comparison by shift of where meals are being eaten and the proportion of time spent "snacking" as opposed to eating full meals. However, the smaller amount of total time spent eating by evening and night workers at least initially indicates that working one of these nonstandard shifts could be somewhat detrimental to people's physical health.

Time Spent in Household Activities and Caring for People

Concerns about the health effects of working a nonday schedule center around the notion that working an evening or night shift disrupts the rhythm of life and the timing of normal activities in which most everyone participates. Alternatively, individuals working nonday schedules may have different functional roles within their families than do day workers, and differences in the amount of time spent in various activities by nonday workers may reflect these different roles rather than disruptions caused by the work schedule.

A set of activities that might be particularly reflective of different functional roles are those related to the maintenance of a residence and care of family and friends. Consistent with the existence of different family roles and with evening and night workers playing a larger role in the running of their households, the ATUS estimates in Table 6.2 indicate that nonday workers spent more time in household chores such as cleaning, laundry, preparing food, gardening, and paying bills than did day workers. Night workers, on average, spent about 12 minutes longer on household chores than did day workers, and evening workers spent approximately 6 minutes longer.[6] Interestingly, the larger amount of time spent by nonday workers on household chores was observed for both male and female workers, although, within shifts, women spent more time on household chores than did men. Specifically, among men, day workers spent 43 minutes, evening workers spent 47 minutes, and night workers spent 62 minutes in household chores. Among women, day workers spent 71 minutes, evening workers spent 81 minutes, and night workers spent 89 minutes on household chores.

The amount of time that day, evening, and night workers spent caring for household and nonhousehold members on their workdays was less consistent with the notion that nonday workers were more responsible for running the household and the care of family members. In fact, evening workers were estimated to spend approximately 6 minutes less than day workers caring for others in the household (20 minutes versus 26 minutes), while the amount of time that day and night workers spent per day caring for others was very similar. When the analysis was restricted to parents with children in the household under the age of 18, day and evening workers were estimated to spend the same amount of time caring for household members (49 minutes), while night workers who were parents were estimated to spend only an extra 4 minutes per day caring for household members (53 minutes).

Time Spent Purchasing Goods and Services

Differences in the amount of time workers on various schedules spend purchasing goods and services also could be reflective of different functional roles in the family. However, to the extent that people can shop only when stores are open, different amounts of time spent shopping could indicate disruptions caused by nonday schedules.

The estimates in Table 6.2 do not support the hypothesis that working a nonday schedule prevents people from spending time shopping. When time spent purchasing consumer goods, professional and personal care services, and household services is combined, the ATUS estimates indicate that evening workers spent almost four minutes longer and night workers spent almost eight minutes longer purchasing goods and services than did day workers. Perhaps the slightly larger amount of time spent shopping by evening and night workers is related to these workers having to spend more time shopping because they are not able to shop at conveniently grouped or efficiently laid out places. However, the estimates of the time spent on household chores and care for friends and family suggest that the increased time spent shopping by nonday workers is probably more indicative of differing household responsibilities. It also could indicate that households with members on different schedules optimally choose to have someone shop when stores are less crowded. At a minimum, these ATUS estimates do not seem to suggest that working a nonday schedule unduly disrupts the purchase of goods and services.

Time Spent in Leisure, "Free" Time Activities

Individuals can spend their nonwork free time in a myriad of ways, and it can be difficult to choose how to group these activities together. In this section the amount of time individuals spent socializing, relaxing, and in leisure activities is combined with the time individuals spent in volunteer and religious activities. Examination of the total amount of time workers spend in these leisure, "free" time activities will provide insights into whether working a nonday schedule infringes on workers' ability to relax and spend time in pleasurable nonwork activities. Differences in specific activities under the broad rubric of leisure time activities are also examined so as to obtain additional clues into whether someone has to alter activities to fit a nonday schedule. For example, for workers to devote part of their socializing and leisure time to attending parties or volunteering at their children's schools, they need to synchronize their schedules with the relevant segments of society, while relatively little coordination is necessary for an individual to watch TV.

The ATUS estimates in Table 6.2 indicate that night workers spent approximately 38 more minutes in leisure time activities on the days that they worked than did day or evening workers. But, all workers, regardless of their shift, spent a large proportion of their leisure time watching television, with night workers spending a slightly larger fraction of their relaxation time watching television than other types of workers. On days that they worked, night workers on average spent 2.1 hours watching television, which is approximately 23 minutes more than day workers and 31 minutes more than evening workers spent watching television. If time spent watching TV is removed, then the amounts of time day, evening, and night workers spent in leisure activities were more comparable. However, even excluding time spent watching television, night workers were still estimated to spend 11 more minutes, and evening workers were estimated to spend 8 more minutes in leisure time activities than were day workers.

Given the estimates in this subsection, it is clear that in general one's overall assessment of what the different amounts of time that day, evening, and night workers spent in leisure time activities indicate about the ability of individuals on nonday schedules to integrate into society and the cost of working a nonday schedule largely hinges on one's feelings about television viewing. Evening and night workers spent slightly more time in leisure time activities when time watching TV was excluded, which could indicate that working a nonstandard schedule could facilitate participating in leisure time activities on work days. Still more than half of workers' leisure time, regardless of their shift, was spent watching television. To the extent that watching television is a pleasurable, restful activity, the finding that night workers spent more time viewing television compared to workers on other shifts suggests that working a night schedule actually increases the amount of time workers spend unwinding and relaxing. On the other hand, to the extent that watching television compensates night workers for other activities in which they are not able to participate, the greater amount of TV viewing by night workers would not be completely positive.

Time Spent in Other, Selected Activities

Among the wide variety of activities in which individuals can participate during the course of the day, some might be considered primarily self-improving investments in oneself, while others might be considered primarily nuisance activities that have to be engaged in as a part of the society in which we live. Educational activities fall into the first category, while time spent traveling to, from, and for work tends to fall into the latter category.

The estimates in Table 6.2 show particularly dramatic differences in the amount of time evening workers spent in educational activities compared to night and day workers. On average, on days that they also worked, evening workers spent approximately 49 minutes in educational activities, which includes attending classes either for a degree or just for personal interest. In contrast, both day and night workers, including those who did not participate in educational activities at all, spent less than 10 minutes in educational activities. The dramatically larger amount of time evening workers spent in educational activities reflects at least in part the fact that a significantly larger proportion of evening workers were enrolled in school than were either day or night workers. However, when the sample is restricted to just those enrolled in school, evening workers were still estimated to spend significantly more time in educational activities than day workers (177 minutes versus 53 minutes).[7]

Consistent with there being more traffic congestion during standard rush hour times, both evening and night workers were estimated to spend less time traveling to work compared to day workers. On average, day workers were estimated to spend 42 minutes commuting to and from work (or in other work-related travel), while evening workers spent 35 minutes and night workers spent a little more than 32 minutes in work-related travel.

The differences in the amount of time spent in educational activities and work-related travel by those on nonday schedules compared to day workers could be indicative of the benefits of working an evening or night shift. Specifically, working an evening schedule could free up time to attend classes and participate in educational activities when they are often offered, thus making obtaining a postsecondary degree economically feasible for some individuals. A reduction in commuting time to work could allow more time for other more productive or enjoyable activities and perhaps could reduce the stress involved in commuting.

Overall, the estimates of the amount of time individuals on different shifts spend in various activities do not seem to indicate that working either an evening or a night shift is particularly disruptive of the normal activities of individuals' lives or their integration into society, with perhaps the exception of the amount of time spent eating. Indeed, at least on their work days, the evidence presented in this section indicates that working an atypical shift may be slightly beneficial to workers given that evening and night workers spend somewhat more time in leisure time activities and less time commuting. Many of the other differences in the amount of time that day, evening, and night workers spend on various activities seem more reflective of the different functional roles these workers may have within their households rather than an intrinsic effect of working a nonday schedule.

TIME SPENT INTERACTING WITH OTHERS

The previous section found that individuals on evening and night shifts spent close to the same amount of time in various activities as day workers. However, this by itself does not necessarily imply that workers on atypical schedules are well integrated into society and that they are not bearing undue costs from working a nonday schedule. For example, a night worker could spend an hour alone eating and another hour alone playing solitaire, whereas a day worker could spend an hour eating with his children and an hour playing cards with his wife. One of these workers might be considered to be quite isolated from society, while the other might be considered well integrated. The estimate of the amount of time spent in an activity provides no indication of whether the activity was done jointly with others or at least with other people around.

To address concerns about the ability of evening and night workers to interact with others and correspondingly their potential estrangement from society, this section examines estimates of the average amount of time workers on various schedules spent alone, with friends, with a spouse (if married), and with their children (if a parent with a child under age 18 in the household). To account for possible relationships between the characteristics of workers and the amount of time they spent interacting with others, and demographic differences in the workers on various shifts, multivariate regression models also were estimated.[8] However, these multivariate results are not presented or discussed in the text unless they suggest that the findings observed in the descriptive statistics are largely due to the differing characteristics of workers on various shifts. The total amount of time individuals spent alone and interacting with others provides another measure of the potential differential cost of being a nonday worker.

160 Polivka

Time Spent Alone

The summary estimates in Table 6.3 indicate that working an evening or night shift might increase people's isolation from society, since workers on both of these shifts were estimated to spend more time alone. Compared to day workers, night workers on average spent almost 40 more minutes alone on days that they worked, while evening workers spent almost 60 more minutes alone. Even married night and evening workers were estimated to spend 31 and 41 more minutes alone, respectively, than married day workers. The additional time evening and night workers spent alone represents a considerable proportion of the time these workers were awake and not working. Evening workers were estimated to spend 48 percent of such hours alone, while night workers were estimated to spend 45 percent of this time alone. In comparison, day workers were estimated to spend 40 percent of the time that they were not working or asleep by themselves.

Time Spent with Friends

The summary estimates in Table 6.3 indicate that evening workers spent approximately 19 more minutes in the company of friends than did day workers, while night workers spent approximately 12 minutes

Table 6.3 Hours Spent in the Company of Others, by Worker's Shift

Variables	All	Day shift	Evening shift	Night shift
Time alone	3.46	3.33	4.23	3.95
Time with friends	0.51	0.46	0.77	0.66
Time with family members	2.76	2.84	2.02	3.11
Time with spouse (if spouse present in the household)	2.75	2.79	2.04	3.16
Time alone with spouse (if spouse present in the household)	1.66	1.68	1.31	1.73
Time with children (if parent and a child is in the household)	3.02	2.96	3.02	4.07
Time with children (including siblings, if a child is in the household)	2.86	2.87	2.44	3.64

more with friends. However, in the multivariate analysis that included controls for other factors, night workers were not estimated to spend significantly more time with friends, while evening workers were estimated to spend significantly less time with friends than comparable day workers. The difference between the summary descriptive statistics and the multivariate analysis controlling for other factors reflects the fact that, on average, those enrolled in school, younger workers, and those working part time were estimated to spend more time with friends. The estimates in Table 6.1 indicate that evening workers were more likely to possess each of these characteristics. Therefore, the multivariate analysis implies that there is nothing intrinsic per se about working an evening schedule that would encourage or permit individuals to spend more time with friends. Rather, it is the characteristics of those who work evenings that were causing these workers to appear to spend more time with friends. Indeed, the multivariate analysis indicates that compared to similar day workers, working an evening schedule disrupts workers' ability to interact with their friends.

Time Spent with Children

The estimates presented earlier, in the section titled "Comparison of the Activities of Day, Evening, and Night Workers," of the amount of time individuals spent in activities related to the care of household members indicate that workers who were parents spent comparable amounts of time caring for other household members regardless of their shifts. However, individuals could be with their children and not be actually involved in an activity that involves caring for them (as defined by the ATUS). For example, if everyone in the family were sitting at the table eating together, the time spent eating reported in Table 6.2 would not be reported as time providing care to family members, nor would it reflect that this was an activity done with others present.

The estimates in Table 6.3 of the amount of time that day, evening, and night workers who were parents had their children physically with them provide a more complete measure of the amount of time parents are aware of and interacting with their children, and a partial measure of the degree of involvement workers on various schedules may have in family life. In turn, the estimates of the amount of time parents spent with their children also could provide hints as to whether individuals on various schedules have different functional roles in the family.

The estimates in Table 6.3 indicate that among parents with children in the household, night workers were estimated to spend significantly more time with their children than day workers. Parents who worked at night were estimated to spend 67 more minutes with their children than day workers. This additional time represents approximately 12 percent of the time night workers were awake and not working. The greater amount of time that parents who worked at night spent with their children existed even when the analysis was restricted to married workers. Married night workers who were parents were estimated to spend a little more than 4 hours with their children on the days that they worked, while married day workers who were parents spent less than 3 hours with their children.

In the aggregate descriptive statistics, evening workers who were parents were estimated to spend approximately the same amount of time with their children as day workers, but in the multivariate analysis, which controls for other factors, evening workers were estimated to spend almost 15 minutes less with their children than comparable day workers. The multivariate analysis also indicates that married evening workers who were parents spent less time with their children than comparable married day workers who were parents, but the evidence is not as strong.[9]

Time Married Workers Spent with Their Spouses

Similar to the estimates of the amount of time workers on various shifts spent with their children, the estimates in Table 6.3 indicate that, compared to married day workers, married night workers spent more time with their spouses, while married evening workers spent less time in the company of their spouses. Night workers who were married spent 22 more minutes with their spouses than did married day workers, although very little of this additional time was spent alone with their spouses (3 minutes).

Married evening workers, in contrast, spent 45 fewer minutes with their spouses than married day workers. Further, the smaller amount of time that evening workers spent with their spouses translated into 22 fewer minutes than married evening workers spent with their spouses alone without anyone else around, compared to married day workers.

Overall, the estimates in this section suggest that working an evening shift, and to a lesser extent a night shift, may reduce an individual's ability to be integrated into society. Evening workers were estimated to spend significantly more time alone, and, controlling for workers' age and school enrollment (among other factors) less time with their friends on the days that they worked. This lack of interaction time seems to indicate that there is a cost to working an evening shift. In addition, the estimates of the amount of time that workers on various shifts spend with family members indicate that being an evening worker may put a strain on family dynamics. Married evening workers were estimated to spend less time with their spouses, while parents who worked an evening shift were estimated to spend less time with their children. The smaller amount of time evening workers spend with their children suggests that evening workers are at home a smaller proportion of the time when their family members are also at home and awake. In turn, this suggests that the reduced time spent with children by parents who work in the evening could reflect a way that families with two individuals in the labor market balance the demands of employment and child care requirements. Whatever the cause, the smaller amount of time evening workers spend with their children and spouses seems to further indicate that working an evening shift is imposing a cost on these workers.

Night workers also were estimated to spend slightly more time alone, which could indicate that these workers are less integrated into society. However, in contrast to evening workers, night workers were estimated to spend significantly more time with their spouses and children than comparable day workers. These estimates suggest that, contrary to some previous research, being a night worker may increase marital stability and raise the quality of family dynamics. At a minimum there is no indication that working a night shift increases the economic cost of employment, at least with regard to the amount of time spent by parents with their children and married individuals with their spouses.

PROPORTION OF TIME WITH OTHERS SPENT IN VARIOUS ACTIVITIES

To obtain an even more complete picture of the degree to which workers are potentially integrated into society, it is important to examine what people are doing when they are together. The assessment of the quality of time people spend together by only examining what they are doing necessarily involves normative judgments. However, the classification of activities such as housecleaning, cooking, and shopping as lower quality and the classification of activities such as eating out, attending parties, and watching television as higher quality is consistent with household production theory and the division of people's time into work, nonmarket work, and leisure (Aguiar and Hurst 2007). For example, using this type of scheme, if an evening worker spent the majority of time with his spouse cleaning house and traveling to and from the grocery store, while a day worker spent the majority of the time with her spouse eating dinner and watching a movie, one would conclude that the "quality" of time that the day worker spent with her spouse was higher than the "quality" of time the evening work spent with his spouse.

To obtain a measure of what individuals were doing when they were in the company of family and friends, and to assess at least partially the quality of this time spent together, the proportion of time that married individuals spent with their spouses and the proportion of time all workers spent with friends in various activities were estimated. To complete the analysis, the proportion of time individuals spent engaged in various activities while alone also was estimated.

Figure 6.1 presents the proportion of time that married workers on different shifts spent with their spouses in various activities, while Figure 6.2 presents the proportion of time spent with friends, and Figure 6.3 presents the proportion of time alone that was spent in various activities. In these figures, any activity that was less than 1 percent was combined into a single Other category, and several related categories were combined into a single broad category. (For example, Consumer Purchases, Purchases of Professional and Personal Care Services, and Purchases of Household Services were combined into a single Purchasing Goods and Services category).[10]

Figure 6.1 Proportion of Time with Spouses in Various Activities (%)

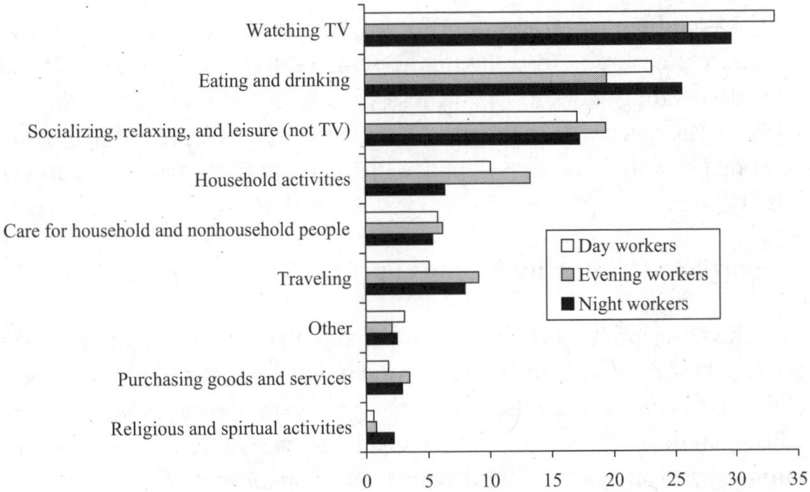

Proportion of Time with Spouses Spent in Various Activities

Examination of the proportion of "spousal time" that workers spent engaged in various activities reveals some interesting and striking differences among workers on various schedules, particularly between evening workers and workers on other schedules. Combining the proportion of time spent in household activities, care for individuals, purchase of goods and services, and travel under the broader rubric of home production, Figure 6.1 indicates that married evening workers spent 32 percent of the time that they were with their spouses engaged in these home production type activities. In contrast, day workers and night workers spent only 23 percent of the time they were with their spouses engaged in these home production activities.[11] Further, the greater proportion of time spent in home production activities primarily came at the expense of activities that generally are considered more pleasurable. Combining the proportion of the time spent with one's spouse in socializing, relaxing, and leisure activities; watching television; and eating and drinking, it is estimated that both day and night workers spent approximately 73 percent of their time with their spouses in such activities, while evening workers spent only 65 percent of the time with their spouses in these more pleasurable activities. The greater proportion of time that evening workers were with their spouses that was spent in home production activities—and the smaller proportion of time together that was spent in primarily pleasurable or relaxing activities—seem to indicate that not only do evening workers spend less time with their spouses than day workers, as was noted in the previous section, but the proportion of the time that evening workers spend with their spouses may be of lower quality.

Proportion of Time with Friends Spent in Various Activities

The descriptive statistics indicate that both evening and night workers spent more time with friends than day workers, but Figure 6.2 indicates that evening and night workers spent a smaller proportion of this additional time in what might be considered enjoyable activities. Combining the proportion of time with friends spent eating and drinking; watching television; socializing, relaxing, and in other leisure activities except watching television; and in sports, exercise, and recreational activities, it is estimated that day workers spent almost 82 percent of their time with friends in these activities, while evening workers spent 77 percent and night workers spent 75 percent of their time with friends in these activities. It also is interesting to note that within this time that was spent with friends in pleasant, enjoyable activities, day workers spent a significantly larger proportion—51 percent—of their time with friends eating compared to evening workers (36 percent) and night workers (32 percent). The smaller proportion of time with their friends that evening and night workers spent eating suggests that working during the dinner time may be disruptive to these workers' socializing. At a minimum, these estimates suggest that working an evening or night schedule requires these workers to spend their time with friends differently than day workers.

Figure 6.2 does indicate, however, that the smaller proportion of time with friends spent in activities that are primarily considered pleasurable is largely offset for evening workers by a larger proportion of time with friends spent in educational activities and for night workers by a larger proportion of time with friends spent in household activities and purchasing goods and services.[12] Since time spent in educational

**Figure 6.2 Proportion of Time with Friends Spent in Various
Activities (%)**

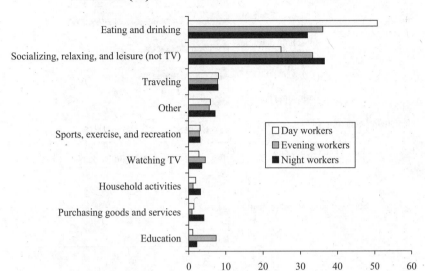

activities can be considered self-improving, and time spent with friends shopping could at least sometimes be considered enjoyable socializing, the differences in the proportion of time with friends that day, night and evening workers spent in various activities do not provide any clear indication that—at least with regards to these proportions—working a nonstandard shift reduces the quality of time spent together.

Proportion of Time Alone Spent in Various Activities

The aggregate estimates indicate that both evening and night workers spent more time alone than day workers. This may indicate that these workers are more isolated from society than day workers. To obtain a better sense of this, it is necessary to examine what day, evening, and night workers were doing during the time they were alone.

Figure 6.3 indicates that a strikingly large proportion of the time individuals were alone was spent traveling to, from, or for work, regardless of their work shift. Figure 6.3 also indicates, however, that evening and night workers spent a smaller proportion of their time alone commuting and traveling for work than did day workers. Day workers on

Figure 6.3 Proportion of Time Alone Spent in Various Activities (%)

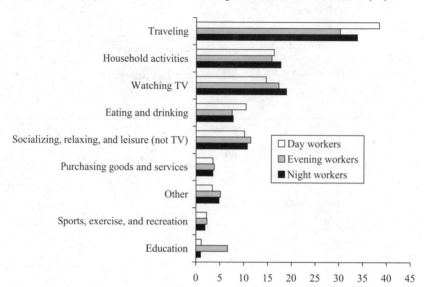

average spent 38 percent of the time that they were alone commuting or in work-related travel. In comparison, evening workers spent 30 percent of their time alone and night workers spent 34 percent of their time alone in work-related travel. The smaller proportion of their time alone that evening workers spent traveling is absorbed, at least partially, by evening workers spending more of their time alone in educational activities and watching television. For night workers, the smaller proportion of time alone that was spent traveling was absorbed by watching TV by oneself. Evening workers spent about 7 percent of the time that they were alone in educational activities compared to only 1 percent of the time day and night workers were alone. Night workers were estimated to spend 19 percent of their time alone watching television, compared to evening workers who spent approximately 17 percent of their time alone watching television and day workers who spent about 15 percent of their time alone this way.

Overall, the estimates in this section do not provide a clear indication of the quality of the increased time that evening and night workers spend alone. Spending more of one's time alone in educational activities indicates that this time alone was being put to good use. The reduction in the proportion of time alone spent commuting and in work-related travel also would imply that the quality of evening and night workers' time alone was higher than that of day workers. The larger proportion of time alone that night and evening workers spent watching television, however, may counteract some of these positive effects, particularly if evening and night workers are watching television alone in lieu of interacting with others.

CONCLUSION

The purpose of this research was to compare how and with whom people on various work shifts spend their time. Information concerning differences in the amount of time spent on certain activities and in interactions with others, and the "quality" of time that people spend together, could help establish whether there is a cost to working a nonday schedule.

The evidence seems to indicate that there is an economic cost to workers and their families of having an evening schedule. For example, evening workers were estimated to spend less time eating than were day workers, which could adversely affect evening workers' health if they more often ate fast food or snacked in lieu of eating a full meal. Probably even more important to their quality of life and family dynamics, evening workers were estimated to spend more time alone, less time with family members (both those residing inside and outside of their households), less time with their spouses if they were married, and less time with their children if they were parents. After controlling for other factors such as a worker's age and whether an individual was enrolled in school, evening workers also were estimated to spend less time with their friends. These estimates indicate that the cost of working an evening schedule could be high.

Further, the estimates indicate that not only did evening workers spend less time with their spouses, but also the quality of time that they did spend together appears to be lower. Compared to married day workers, married evening workers spent a larger proportion of the time they were with their spouses doing what typically are considered to be unpleasant, obligatory home production activities, such as household chores and shopping, and a smaller proportion of their time together in more pleasurable activities, such as eating and drinking, or socializing and relaxing.

The higher costs of working an evening schedule could be partially offset by the finding that evening workers were estimated to spend a larger proportion of their nonwork time in educational activities and less time commuting to, from, or for work. In fact, working an evening schedule may permit some workers to attend school who otherwise might be financially unable to do so. Overall, however, it seems unlikely that the benefits of working an evening schedule completely offset the costs.

In contrast, the costs of working a night schedule do not appear to be as high. On the one hand, night workers were estimated to spend more time alone and less time eating than day workers, both of which suggest that working a night schedule could be somewhat costly and could be indicative of night workers being less well integrated into society. At the same time, the research presented in this chapter indicates that night workers spent less time commuting to work and more time relaxing, although much of this additional relaxation time was spent watching television. In terms of family dynamics, night workers spent more time with their families, particularly their children if they were parents, but also with their spouses if married. The estimates of the proportion of time spent in various activities while with one's spouse also indicate that the "quality" of time that day and night workers spent with their spouses was fairly equivalent. These latter estimates suggest that having a night schedule might decrease some of the costs of working, increase marital stability, and improve family dynamics.

It is important to note that from the research presented in this chapter, it is impossible to determine the amount of time evening or night workers might have spent with their families if they had worked during the day instead. As was hinted at in the discussion of the amount of time workers devoted to household activities, workers on nonday schedules may play a different functional role in their households than do day workers, and working a nonday schedule may be a way for individuals to both fulfill their functional roles within their households and to work. The multivariate analysis briefly discussed here takes into account some of the compositional differences in workers in the various shifts, but to obtain an even broader picture of the costs of working a nonday schedule it is important to explore why workers are working the schedules that they are. Yet another line of research that it will be necessary to undertake to obtain a complete picture is what individuals on various shifts do on their days off, since on workdays the time available for nonwork activities is constrained for all individuals regardless of their shift.

Research done in the 1970s suggests that public laws such as the Fair Labor Standards Act encouraged employers to substitute shift schedules for longer daily or weekly work schedules. This occurred, it is argued, because the laws required employers to pay a wage premium for workweeks and days in excess of prescribed standards, but did not require a premium to be paid for working 8 hours on an evening or night shift (Hedges and Sekscenski 1979). Despite the caveats about the evidence presented here and the advisability of undertaking additional research, the analysis presented in this chapter strongly suggests that if the need for evening and night workers expands with changes in the U.S. economy, consideration should be given to who will accept these jobs and the costs that accepting these jobs might impose on workers and their families.

Notes

The views expressed in this chapter are solely those of the author and do not represent the opinions or policies of the Bureau of Labor Statistics.

1. The ATUS is a continuing survey, but data from subsequent years are not used in this analysis.
2. There were a few instances in which workers did not work at least half of their hours in one of these time intervals or when a worker's time was evenly split between two or three of these intervals. In these instances, workers were coded based on when they worked the majority of their hours, using an algorithm based on their starting and stopping times combined with their duration of work, or in a few rare instances by visual inspection. The few individuals who were observed to work almost continuously around the clock were excluded from the analysis. To avoid issues of potential asymmetry in work duration, for individuals whose last activity was recorded as working, the work event was allowed to extend beyond 4 a.m of the interview day for classification as a day, evening, or night worker. Experimentation indicates that truncating individuals' work hours at 4 a.m. of the

interview day would not substantially alter the proportion of workers classified as day, evening, or night workers.

3. To account for the stratified sample design of the ATUS and the oversampling of blacks, Hispanics, those working on weekends, and those with children, sample weights were used in all of the analysis presented in this chapter.

4. Unpublished work by the author presented at the ATUS Early Results conference in December 2005 (Polivka 2005) indicate that there is a great deal of concordance between the ATUS estimates of the number of wage and salary workers working day, night, and evening shifts and estimates derived from the 2004 supplement to the CPS about individuals' work schedules.

5. To account for the fact that several characteristics could be related (for example, younger workers probably are also more likely to be enrolled in school and less likely to be married or working full time), a standard multinomial logit model where the dependent variable was being either a day, evening, or night worker also was estimated. However, since the coefficient estimates and corresponding estimated marginal effects generated from this multivariate model generally accorded well with the descriptive statistics, the results from the multinomial model are not reported. The multinomial results are available from the author on request.

6. Analysis restricted to full-time workers also indicated that full-time nonday workers spent more time in household activities than day workers who worked full time.

7. These differences could reflect differences in the days of the week individuals are working or the level of schooling; however, multivariate regression analysis controlling for school enrollment, the number of hours worked, and worker's age, among other factors, still indicate that evening workers spend significantly more time in educational activities than do day workers.

8. In the multivariate analysis the total amount of time or the proportion of non-work time individuals spent alone and interacting with friends, spouses, and children were the dependent variables. Variables included in the models as explanatory variables included controls for workers' age, gender, race, educational attainment, marital status, marital status interacted with gender, annual family income, whether an individual was of Hispanic origin, whether an individual was enrolled in school, the presence of children in the household, the number of children in the household and the age of the youngest child if children were present in the household. Some models also included workers' industries and occupations as controls, but the results for the other explanatory variables did not vary much when workers' industries and occupations were included in the model.

9. The evidence is weaker because the coefficient was only statistically significant at an 11 percent level instead of the standard of at least 10 percent, but the lower significance level could be at least partially due to the relatively small sample size of married evening workers with children. When 2003 and 2004 data were combined, there were only 148 (unweighted) married evening workers who had a child under the age of 18.

10. Sixteen observations were deleted from this analysis due to data inconsistencies in the sample.
11. It is important to note that the time married individuals spend in an activity provides no indication of what their spouses were doing at the same time. The ATUS only collects information about what the respondent was doing; it does not collect information about what other individuals who were present were doing. Consequently, it would be incorrect to assume that just because evening workers spent more time in home production activities when they were with their spouses that their spouses were also engaged in home production and that evening workers were thus getting assistance from their spouses in these home production activities.
12. All workers, regardless of their shift, spent approximately 8 percent of the time that they were with their friends traveling to, from, or for work.

References

Aguiar, Mark, and Erik Hurst. 2007. "Measuring Trends in Leisure: The Allocation of Time over Five Decades." *The Quarterly Journal of Economics* 122(3): 969–1006.

Alexander, K.J., and John Spraos. 1956. "Shift Working: An Application of the Theory of the Firm." *The Quarterly Journal of Economics* 70(4): 603–612.

Beers, Thomas M. 2000. "Flexible Schedules and Shift Work: Replacing the '9-to-5' Workday?" *Monthly Labor Review* 123(6): 33–40.

Bianchi, Suzanne, Vanessa Wight, and Sara Raley. 2005. "Maternal Employment and Family Caregiving: Rethinking Time with Children in the ATUS." Unpublished manuscript prepared for the ATUS Early Results conference held in Washington, DC, December 8–9, 2005.

Brown, D. 1975. "Shiftwork: A Survey of the Sociological Implications of Studies of Male Shiftworkers." *Journal of Occupational Psychology* 48: 231–240.

Bryden, G., and J.L. Holdstock. 1973. "Effects of Night Duty on Sleep Patterns of Nurses." *Psychophysiology* 10(1): 36–42.

Connelly, Rachel, and Jean Kimmel. 2008. "The Role of Nonstandard Work Hours in Maternal Care Giving for Young Children." Unpublished manuscript. Brunswick, ME: Bowdoin College; Kalamazoo, MI: Western Michigan University.

Dunham, Randall. 1977. "Shift Work: A Review and Theoretical Analysis." *The Academy of Management Review* 2(4): 624–634.

Hamermesh, Daniel S. 1996. *Workdays, Workhours and Work Schedules: Evidence for the United States and Germany.* Kalamazoo, MI: W.E. Upjohn Institute for Employment Research.

————. 1998. "When We Work." *American Economic Review* 88(2): 321–325.
————. 1999. "The Timing of Work over Time." *The Economic Journal* 109(452): 37–66.
Hedges, J.N., and Edward S. Sekscenski. 1979. "Workers on Late Shifts in a Changing Economy." *Monthly Labor Review* 102(9): 14–22.
Kleitman, Nathaniel. 1963. *Sleep and Wakefulness*. Chicago: University of Chicago Press.
Kostiuk, Peter F. 1990. "Compensating Differentials for Shift Work." *The Journal of Political Economy* 98(5): 1054–1075.
Morgan, James N. 1981. "Child Care When Parents Are Employed." In *Five Thousand American Families: Patterns of Economic Progress*. Vol. 9. S. Hill, D.H. Hill, and J.N. Morgan, eds. Ann Arbor, MI: University of Michigan, Institute for Social Research, pp. 441–456.
Mott, P.E., F.C. Mann, Q. McLoughlin, and D.P. Warwick. 1965. *Shift Work: The Social, Psychological, and Physical Consequences*. Ann Arbor, MI: University of Michigan Press.
Polivka, Anne. 2005. "Shift Work and Participation in Social, Recreational or Exercise Activities." Unpublished manuscript prepared for the ATUS Early Results conference held in Washington, DC, December 8–9, 2005.
Presser, Harriet B. 1986. "Shift Work among American Women and Child Care." *Journal of Marriage the Family* 48(3): 551–563.
————. 1988. "Shift Work and Child Care among Young Dual-Earner American Parents." *Journal of Marriage and the Family* 50(1): 133–148.
————. 1994. "Employment Schedules Among Dual-Earner Spouses and the Division of Household Labor by Gender." *American Sociological Review* 59(3): 348–364.
————. 1995. "Job, Family, and Gender: Determinants of Nonstandard Work Schedules Among Employed Americans in 1991." *Demography* 32(4): 577–598.
Presser, Harriet B., and Janet C. Gornick. 2005. "The Female Share of Weekend Employment: A Study of 16 Countries." *Monthly Labor Review* 128(8): 41–53.
Rapoport, Benoit, and Celine LeBourdais. Forthcoming. "Parental Time and Working Schedules." *Journal of Population Economics*.
Staines, Graham L., and Joseph H. Pleck. 1984. "Non-Standard Work Schedules and Family Life." *Journal of Applied Psychology* 69: 515–523.
————. 1986. "Work Schedule Flexibility and Family Life." *Journal of Occupational Behaviour* 7(2): 147–153.
Tasto, Donald L., Michael J. Colligan, Eric W. Skjei, and Susan J. Polly. 1978. *Health Consequences of Shift Work*. Contract no. 210-75-0072. Final Report to the National Institute for Occupational Safety and Health.

U.S. Department of Labor. 2005. "Workers on Flexible and Shift Schedules in May 2004." Press release, July 1.

White, Lynn, and Bruce Keith. 1990. "The Effect of Shift Work on the Quality and Stability of Marital Relations." *Journal of Marriage and the Family* 52(2): 453–462.

Wight, Vanessa R., Sara B. Raley, and Suzanne M. Bianchi. 2007. "Time for Children, One's Spouse, and Oneself among Parents Who Work Nonstandard Hours." Unpublished manuscript. College Park, MD: University of Maryland. Earlier version under different title prepared for presentation at the 2006 annual meeting of the Population Association of America.

Zedeck, Sheldon, Susan E. Jackson, and Elizabeth Summers. 1983. "Shift Work Schedules and Their Relationship to Health Adaptation, Satisfaction, and Turnover Intention." *The Academy of Management Journal* 26(2): 297–310.

The Authors

W. Keith Bryant is professor emeritus of policy analysis and management at Cornell University.

Nancy Folbre is professor of economics at the University of Massachusetts, Amherst.

Daniel S. Hamermesh is the Edward Everett Hale Centennial Professor at the University of Texas at Austin, a research fellow with the Institute for the Study of Labor, and a research associate with the National Bureau of Economic Research.

Jean Kimmel is professor of economics at Western Michigan University and a research fellow with the Institute for the Study of Labor.

Anne Polivka is a supervisory senior research economist at the Bureau of Labor Statistics.

Jay Stewart is a research economist at the Bureau of Labor Statistics.

Jennifer Ward-Batts is an assistant professor of economics at Wayne State University.

Jayoung Yoon is an associate professor of economics at the University of Massachusetts, Amherst.

Cathleen D. Zick is professor of family and consumer studies at the University of Utah.

Index

The italic letters *f, n,* and *t* following a page number indicate that the subject information of the heading is within a figure, note, or table, respectively, on that page.

Age
 before and after retirement, in time
  use studies, 7, 21–22, 22*t,* 84–85,
  131
 shift workers and, 148*t*
Aging population, 59, 61, 84–85
Agriculture, shift workers in, 149*t,* 150*t*
American Time Use Survey (ATUS), 2,
  29, 65
 as adult-centric, 32, 44, 53*n*2
 child care codes for, 38–39, 40–41,
  51–53
 data from, 1–2, 3, 4, 8, 9*n*1, 11, 39*t,*
  63–64, 84, 88, 111, 141, 171*n*1,
  172*n*4
 equating TUESA sociodemographics
  with, 68–72
 participants in, 1, 9*n*1
 responses to, 2, 63
Attitudes, 33
 about time and economics, 25–26
 child care quality, 45, 46
ATUS. *See* American Time Use Survey
Australia, 34, 36
 time stress in, 26–27, 26*t,* 28*ff*

BLS. *See* U.S. Bureau of Labor Statistics
Business services, shift workers in, 150*t*

Canada, child care in, 34, 36, 144
Care continuum, 32, 35, 39*t,* 40–43, 42*t,*
  49, 53*n*6
 density of care and, 44, 45–46, 49,
  53*n*7
 wages in, 46, 47*t*
Caregiving
 gender differences on time used for,
  2, 13–15, 13*t,* 14*t,* 15*t*
 as human capital investment, 4, 44
 monetary value and, 4–5, 9*n*2

by nonworking men, 110*f,* 113*t,* 114*t*
 retirement and, 90*t,* 94*t,* 96*t,* 98*t,* 100*t*
 shift workers and, 8, 151, 152*t,* 165*f*
 working mothers and, 3–4
Caregiving categories, 4
 See also Care continuum
CDS-PSID. *See* Child Development
  Supplement of the Panel Study of
  Income Dynamics
Child care, 31–53
 ATUS codes for, 38–39, 40–41, 51–53
 defining time for, 35–43
 estimating market value of time for,
  43–49
 future research on, 49
 gender differences in time for, 14, 14*t*
 market substitutes for, 44–45
 mothers and, 3, 4, 35
 nonworkers and, 111, 121*t,* 123*t*
 parents and, 34–36
 reasons to measure time for, 32–35
 valuing unpaid work of, vs.
  housework, 31–32
 work timing of couples and, 25, 144
 See also Care continuum
Child Development Supplement of the
  Panel Study of Income Dynamics
  (CDS-PSID), 34, 44, 53*n*2
Children, 39
 average number, per family, 14, 60
 money spent on, 33–34
 as public goods, 4, 32–33
 shift workers and, 149*t,* 160*t,* 161–
  162
Civic obligations, shift workers and, 152*t*
Computer ownership, 74–75
Construction, shift workers in, 149*t,* 150*t*
Consumables
 consumption during retirement, 6–7,
  81–83, 85–88

179

186   Kimmel

U.S. Health and Retirement Study
(HRS), data set, 83
Universal child care, 34
Unpaid work
as composite activity of ATUS, 2
definitions of, 5–6, 7, 8, 13, 58, 138n2
"in your care" time as, 37–40, 53n4
(see also Child care)
transfer from, to purchased good, 4
USDA. See U.S. Department of
Agriculture
Utilities, shift workers in, 149t

Vacations, 15, 20–21
Volunteerism
ATUS response rates and, 2
before and after retirement, 90t
retirement and, 94t, 96t, 98t, 100t
shift workers and, 152t
as unpaid work, 58

Wages
care continuum and, 46, 47t
education and, 74
effect on leisure with spouses, 24–25,
24t
housework and, 64, 65, 76nn2–3
opportunity cost of, 9n2, 76n1
premium, and shift work, 142, 171
sleep time and, 2, 17–18, 17t
Weekdays, work times on, compared
internationally, 20, 20t
Weekends, work times on, compared
internationally, 2–3, 20–21, 20t
Wholesale trade, shift workers in, 149t
Women
education-level changes and, 59, 60
time stress of, 27, 28f
time use by, in retirement, 94t–95t,
96t–97t
See also Working women
Work, 2, 3–4, 33
Work timing, 18–25, 18f, 19f
economic costs of, 142
social interaction and, 8–9

spouse's, and leisure synchronicity, 3,
24–25
See also Shift work studies
Working men
living arrangements and income of,
vs. nonworkers, 116t
time stress and, 27, 28f
total work of, 2
work timing for, 18f
Working women
Child care services by, 32, 46–47, 48
labor force participation by, 59, 60,
61, 62
mothers as, 3, 4, 35
sleep and wages of, 17–18
time stress and, 3–4, 26t, 27
total work of, compared
internationally, 15
traditional work of, 2, 5
work timing for, 19f
Workplaces, shift workers and time at,
153t

About the Institute

The W.E. Upjohn Institute for Employment Research is a nonprofit research organization devoted to finding and promoting solutions to employment-related problems at the national, state, and local levels. It is an activity of the W.E. Upjohn Unemployment Trustee Corporation, which was established in 1932 to administer a fund set aside by Dr. W.E. Upjohn, founder of The Upjohn Company, to seek ways to counteract the loss of employment income during economic downturns.

The Institute is funded largely by income from the W.E. Upjohn Unemployment Trust, supplemented by outside grants, contracts, and sales of publications. Activities of the Institute comprise the following elements: 1) a research program conducted by a resident staff of professional social scientists; 2) a competitive grant program, which expands and complements the internal research program by providing financial support to researchers outside the Institute; 3) a publications program, which provides the major vehicle for disseminating the research of staff and grantees, as well as other selected works in the field; and 4) an Employment Management Services division, which manages most of the publicly funded employment and training programs in the local area.

The broad objectives of the Institute's research, grant, and publication programs are to 1) promote scholarship and experimentation on issues of public and private employment and unemployment policy, and 2) make knowledge and scholarship relevant and useful to policymakers in their pursuit of solutions to employment and unemployment problems.

Current areas of concentration for these programs include causes, consequences, and measures to alleviate unemployment; social insurance and income maintenance programs; compensation; workforce quality; work arrangements; family labor issues; labor-management relations; and regional economic development and local labor markets.